ECONOMIC SANCTIONS AND
INTERNATIONAL ENFORCEMENT

The Royal Institute of International Affairs is an unofficial body which promotes the scientific study of international questions and does not express opinions of its own. The opinions expressed in this publication are the responsibility of the author.

The Institute and its Research Committee are grateful for the comments and suggestions made by Professor James Barber and Professor James Fawcett, who were asked to review the manuscript of this book.

ECONOMIC SANCTIONS AND INTERNATIONAL ENFORCEMENT

Margaret P. Doxey, B.Sc. (Econ), Ph.D.

Published for
THE ROYAL INSTITUTE OF
INTERNATIONAL AFFAIRS

© Royal Institute of International Affairs 1971, 1980

All rights reserved. No part of this publication may be
reproduced or transmitted, in any form or by any means,
without permission

First edition (Oxford University Press) 1971
Second edition (Macmillan) 1980

Published by
THE MACMILLAN PRESS LTD
London and Basingstoke
Companies and representatives
throughout the world

Printed in Great Britain by
Billing and Sons Ltd
Guildford, London, Oxford, Worcester

British Library Cataloguing in Publication Data

Doxey, Margaret Pamela
    Economic sanctions and international enforcement.
    – 2nd ed.
    1. Sanctions (International law)
    I. Title   II. Royal Institute of International
    Affairs
    382.1   JX1246

    ISBN 0–333–25707–3

Contents

Preface to the Second Edition

Nearly ten years have elapsed since the first edition of this book was published and although the main lines of argument are still valid, several of the case studies needed updating and new and important developments in the use of collective economic pressure required attention and analysis. In particular, the Southern African situation underwent radical change in the 1970s, while the Arab oil embargo of 1973 provided a dramatic new instance of the collective use of economic weapons to influence the behaviour of states.

My object was and is to provide a succinct and comprehensive treatment of the subject of international economic sanctions. In-depth accounts of the economic effects of sanctions on the various targets have not been attempted, but in the Select Bibliography readers' attention is directed to works which can fill this need.

In preparing the new edition I have again been fortunate to enjoy the unfailing helpfulness and courtesy of the librarians and staff of Chatham House and the Canadian Institute of International Affairs. I am grateful to Trent University for supporting my research, and to Teresa Goncalves who gave invaluable help in typing the manuscript.

Trent University   Margaret Doxey
Ontario
October 1979

1 The Scope of the Inquiry

This study is concerned with the collective exercise of coercion by economic means and particularly with the recourse to international economic sanctions. The subject is one of considerable and continuing interest: United Nations sanctions against Rhodesia (renamed Zimbabwe-Rhodesia in 1979) have been in force since 1966; an arms embargo was imposed on South Africa in 1977; the Arab oil-producing countries made dramatic use of the 'oil weapon' in 1973; Cuba was subjected to OAS sanctions for over a decade. When are economic sanctions justified? Can they work? What costs do they carry? These are some of the questions this book seeks to answer.

Rhodesia, which became the object of mandatory UN sanctions in December 1966, provides a major case study. For a decade the programme of economic deprivation applied by UN members served as the main instrument of external pressure on the government of Ian Smith which declared unilateral independence (UDI) from Britain in 1965. These sanctions were progressively extended in scope by the Security Council and are still officially in force, but their efficacy has been revealed as limited. Over the past few years the incursions into Rhodesia of the guerrilla forces of the Patriotic Front have made military force the prime instrument for change, and the Rhodesian government has become responsive to heavy diplomatic pressure from Western powers and from South Africa which in the early years following UDI was Rhodesia's firm – and crucial – supporter. Concessions from the minority regime produced the internal settlement of 3 March 1978 and led to the election of a black majority in the Rhodesian Parliament and a government led by a black Prime Minister in May 1979. Further modifications in the Rhodesian constitution were proposed by Britain at a conference attended by members of the Rhodesian government and leaders of the Patriotic Front in September. It remains to be seen whether other members of the Commonwealth and the UN will be satisfied with the progress made towards majority rule in Rhodesia and will formally authorize the lifting of collective sanctions. At the time of writing there is no evidence that the guerrilla war is over, full recognition of Rhodesia as an independent state is not in sight, and confident predictions about the future course of events in Central Africa cannot be made. But even if economic sanctions proved ineffective as instruments of change and have now been overtaken by events, their usefulness both in terms of their effects on the target as well as their record of implementation deserves careful evaluation. A great deal of material is now available for this purpose in spite of the interest of all parties to clandestine transactions in keeping their sanctions-evading operations secret.

A shorter-lived but perhaps more dramatic instance of collective economic coercion occurred in 1973 when world attention was focussed on the Middle East, not only because of renewed fighting between Israel and its Arab neighbours, but because of the production cutbacks and embargoes on oil supplies implemented by the Arab oil-producing states. The 'oil weapon' made headlines everywhere and although the embargoes lasted no more than a few months, they created shortages and a new climate of apprehension in consumer countries which, combined with the ensuing massive climb in oil prices, significantly affected their foreign and domestic policies.

In addition to Rhodesia and the Arab oil embargoes, there are several other exercises in collective coercion which merit examination. In the inter-war period, members of the League of Nations placed restraints on their trade with Italy in an effort to deal with the crisis produced by the Italian invasion of Ethiopia and this early experiment in international economic pressure is still of interest. There is also the experience of the second world war in which techniques of economic warfare were considerably developed and refined, and of the ensuing cold war when western powers placed strategic embargoes on trade with communist countries in Europe and the Far East. In the post-war period too, there have been a number of regionally sponsored programmes of economic denial. The Soviet Union, supported by other communist countries, has at different times used economic weapons, particularly against Yugoslavia and Albania, while in the Western Hemisphere restrictions on trade and diplomatic relations with Cuba were imposed by the Organization of American States (OAS) in 1964, and remained in place until 1975. Moreover, three decades of Arab boycotts of Israel, which have had secondary ramifications affecting Israel's economic relations with other countries, preceded the imposition of restrictions on supplies of oil to the US, Western Europe and Japan in 1973–74.

The use of economic weapons to achieve political ends is, of course, not a new phenomenon. They have regularly supplemented the use of force in war and they have been used overtly and covertly to influence the foreign or domestic policy of target states. A wide variety of objectives has been sought: ideological, political and economic. In the twentieth century, the nationalization of foreign assets has often provoked strong reactions from dispossessed corporations and they have generally received support from their home governments, especially where compensation has been withheld or deemed inadequate. Examples are the boycott of Mexican oil following nationalization of its oil industry in 1938; the heavy pressures exerted by Britain and the international oil companies on the government of Dr. Musaddiq to counter the nationalization of assets of the Anglo-Iranian Oil Company in 1951; and the reactions of US multinational corporations, and particularly ITT, first to the prospect and then to the reality of Dr. Allende's election as President of Chile in 1970[1]. But the idea of international sanctions, measures to be used by international bodies to uphold standards of behaviour expected by custom or required by law, is rather different. Sanctions are familiar conformity-defending instruments in national societies; in the social context they may be positive (rewards) or negative (punishments) but in legal systems they are penalties which designated authorities apply to law-breakers. The extension of the concept of authorized enforcement to international society belongs to the twentieth century.[2] It was closely linked with schemes for collective security and the prevention of war, and was first given formal expression with the establishment of the League of Nations. The League Council provided for coercive measures of a military and non-military nature to be collectively imposed by League members in a limited range of situations to enforce conformity with standards of conduct for which the organization had assumed continuing responsibility and which were generally accepted by members of international society as worthy of support. The United Nations Charter gave even greater emphasis to the enforcement process which was to be activated and administered by the Security Council. Measures ordered by the Security Council for the maintenance of international peace and security are mandatory for members in terms of Article 25 and are correctly described as sanctions, although the veto means that none of the permanent members can be subjected to them without its consent. In cases of suspension of the rights and privileges of membership (Article 5) or expulsion (Article 6), a General Assembly resolution also has binding force provided it is backed by a recommendation from the Security Council, but the status of measures which are *recommended* by the Security Council or by the General Assembly is less clear. They may be considered 'authorized' but they are not mandatory.[3] As the General Assembly votes by a two-thirds majority on any substantive matter and is not restricted by the veto power, it can express the majority view in respect of the conduct of any member of the UN, large or small. States (governments) which vote for its resolutions could be expected to apply them; others are encouraged, but not bound to do so.[4] Measures of this kind are often described as voluntary or optional sanctions, and in view of the decentralized nature of world society, with state sovereignty as its main structural feature, this is a reasonable convention.

Other international bodies also have sanctioning powers. Specialized agencies in the United Nations system which are concerned with functional co-operation in such areas as economic and monetary policy, health, transport and communication, may be able to control their own membership (although in some cases it is linked directly with United Nations membership) and can impose sanctions in this respect. They may also be able to deny other privileges, such as access to services or resources. The grounds for such penalties are usually non-payment of budgetary contributions, but other offences may be specified. For instance, the International Monetary Fund (IMF) and the World Bank can suspend a member for a general breach of obligations, while GATT, in terms of Article 23, provides for ultimate collective authorization of retaliatory measures, after exhaustion of other means of settlement, if a member has failed to fulfil its obligations.[5] In addition, the agreements linking the United Nations and certain agencies, including the International Labour Organization (ILO), the Food and Agriculture Organization (FAO), and the International Civil Aviation Organization (ICAO), require them to assist the Security Council in carrying out enforcement decisions when requested to do so. The IMF and the World Bank, on the other hand, are prohibited in their articles of agreement from engaging in political activity of any kind and are required only to give 'due regard' to decisions of the Security Council.[6]

Regional economic associations, such as the European Economic Community (EEC) may also make provision for internal sanctions: they control their own membership and may be authorized by the founding treaty or agreement to impose penalties for failure to observe obligations.[7] The test in all these cases is whether the organization is constitutionally empowered to take disciplinary action and whether the measures it takes against a member are linked to a failure to observe standards of behaviour defined in relevant agreements.

Regional political organizations present more difficult problems especially where they claim a legitimate role in maintaining international peace and security. Resort to the threat or use of force outside the framework of UN authorization is prohibited by Article 2(4) of the Charter, with individual and collective self-defence in terms of Article 51 the only exception. The Charter provided for control of the activities of regional bodies in Chapter VIII: any recourse to enforcement action was to be subject to Security Council authorization. In practice, this control has been non-existent and consequently one enters rather a 'grey' area in considering the legality of activities of such bodies as the OAS, the Arab League, and the Organization for African Unity (OAU), which are recognized regional arrangements in terms of Chapter VIII. If members of these bodies seek to discipline their fellow members by political ostracization, programmes of economic denial, and even the use of military force, are they engaged in sanctioning? For instance the majority of OAS members voted to exclude Cuba from participation in the organization because they deemed its Marxist-Leninist government to be incompatible with the prevailing capitalist ideology of the western hemisphere and imposed econ-omic embargoes because of that government's perceived inter-ference in the affairs of other Latin American states. Although the OAS asserted that it was not taking 'enforcement action' against Cuba, it is clear that penalties were being imposed. Questions may also be raised about action by the North Atlantic Treaty or Warsaw Pact countries, allied for collective self-defence. Did the invasion of Czechoslovakia by the Warsaw Pact Countries under Soviet leadership qualify for the status of a military sanction? The Brezhnev doctrine, enunciated after the invasion, certainly asserted a group right to uphold the norms of the Socialist commonwealth.[8]

A further problem relates to the nature of the measures used. There has not been consensus on the question whether economic coercion is included in the meaning of 'force' under Article 2(4) of the Charter. Bowett notes that in discussions preceding the drafting of the UN Declaration on Friendly Relations the western powers supported a narrow interpretation of Article 2(4) restricting it to military force while others, including some Eastern European states and Egypt, wanted economic aggression to be included.[9] In the final form of the Declaration, adopted without vote in October 1970, economic coercion is dealt with under the (third) principle of non-intervention (the first two being the non-use of force and the peaceful settlement of disputes).[10] But the wording of the clause in the Declaration is absurdly vague: "No State may use or encourage the use of economic, political or any other type of measures to coerce another state in order to obtain from it the subordination of the exercise of its sovereign rights and to secure from it advantages of any kind." As Bowett points out, economic coercion would already have been illegal if it violated bilateral or multilateral treaty commitments, or general principles of international law such as the freedom of the seas.[11] It may now be viewed as illegal under the rubric of intervention, but charges of this kind can and no doubt will be countered by justification of action in terms of domestic economic needs. And the principle of state sovereignty protects the right of governments to take steps to develop and protect their chosen economic systems, and to conserve their own resources.[12]

Beauty may be in the eye of the beholder, but there is little doubt that coercion and intervention are in the eye of the coerced. While external powers will normally seek to give their acts a cloak of legality and legitimacy by pointing to norms established by international agreement which they claim it is their duty to uphold, the object of the exercise may have a different view. And whereas direct military intervention is easier to discern than supportive practices such as supplying arms, bases and training, economic intervention may be much more difficult to identify. The lack of overall authority at the United Nations level leaves the victim no channels for appeal. Thus, where there is a regional agreement in force which establishes certain standards for signatories, and if there is a constitutionally taken decision that one of them is failing to live up to these standards and must be collectively disciplined, then the majority will probably consider that they are applying sanctions and it is acceptable to use the term to describe the measures employed. This is a subjective interpretation and begs the question of how the victim – and how extra-regional powers –

view their action. It is also possible that some of the members themselves may have been coerced into support for collective action by a dominant power in the region. The two superpowers have generally been prepared to leave each other a free hand in acknowledged spheres of influence – such as Latin America and Eastern Europe – and this leaves regional sanctioning unchallenged if other members of the regional group are supportive of superpower policy.

Interestingly enough, neither the League Covenant nor the UN Charter used the word 'sanction' and a rather loose usage of the term is no doubt unavoidable in contemporary society, but it is both useful and important to distinguish between authorized measures, whether mandatory or optional, which are based on the decision or recommendation of an international body, and non-authorized measures, justified by those who take them (whether unilaterally or in concert) as self-defence or as reprisals. These distinctions will be adhered to in the chapters that follow.[13]

Self-defence, in the face of armed attack, is permitted by the Charter and governments regularly cite self-defence as justification for economic measures which might otherwise be illegal. For instance, the Arab oil embargoes were stated to be defensive.[14] Less susceptible to sweeping claims of justifiability perhaps are reprisals taken in retaliation for an earlier, illegal act for which other means of redress have been exhausted or are not available, and which are proportionate to the offence. As Bowett points out unilateral reprisals differ substantially from "collective organizational action conceived as a sanction" which involves the concept of "community action" to deal with a threat to or breach of the peace.[15] But action can also be depicted as collective reprisals, which may be harder to categorize. It is certain that unless survival is at stake peaceful means of settlement should be resorted to before any coercive measures are employed, but in international relations, in the absence of an authoritative ruling as to whether the law has, in fact, been broken and of a consensus for action which would make unilateral reprisals unnecessary, states are left to protect their own interests.

The cases noted at the beginning of this chapter provide important material for evaluating the modalities and efficacy of collective economic coercion. It is important, too, to note that on the spectrum of persuasion-coercion, there are other non-violent measures which have been used as sanctions. Diplomatic and political sanctions have been widely utilized in recent years and the exclusion of certain states from participation in the activities of international organizations has been sedulously pursued by others as a form of international punishment.

Chapters 2 to 5 give short accounts of the various programmes of economic denial mentioned above, which in turn, provide a basis for analysing the processes of international coercion. Chapters 6 and 7 deal with specific problems of organizing collective measures and with the reaction of target states. For sanctionists, there is the crucial question of consensus which affects all stages of the international decision-making process: the need to define goals, the selection of particular measures in relation to the vulnerability of the target, and the cost factor. Of equal importance is the response of the target in meeting the challenge of external pressure: defence of the economy and its performance under stress; an examination of the influences which affect opinion and conduct among its citizens; the extent of outside help, and the development of new industrial and commercial patterns which may result from the blocking of previous channels of supply and exchange.

In a short study it is impossible to provide any detailed economic analysis of the effect of sanctions or other coercive measures on the economies of targets. There is in any case, a serious methodological problem in attempting any precise measurement of the effects of sanctions. It is not possible to isolate them from the effects of other factors which may be operating to reinforce their impact, nor can there always be confident assertion about what the behaviour of the target state would have been if no sanctions had been threatened or imposed. But political effects, or non-effects, are often discernible and general conclusions may be drawn. The concluding chapter serves as a summary of findings. It also considers the utility of international political sanctions which involve exclusion from participation or membership in international organizations.

2 Economic Warfare in the 20th Century

Theoretically, as noted in the previous chapter, there are important differences in the status and purpose of economic measures used as techniques of warfare, either in conjunction with military measures or independently, and economic sanctions employed by an international organization as part of a constitutionally authorized enforcement process. In conditions of war, the target is the enemy; the objective is to hasten its defeat, to reduce or eliminate its capacity to wage war, and to undermine morale. Humanitarian considerations may play some part, but destruction of life and property are priorities of war. When economic measures are used as sanctions, the objective should be to deter or dissuade states from pursuing policies which do not conform to accepted norms of international conduct. Compliance is considered to be in the general interest, and sanctions are penalties which relate specifically to acts which the international body condemns. Unnecessary hardship is to be avoided.

There are, however, obvious similarities between sanctions and economic warfare: the weapons are drawn from the same armoury and problems of application will be common to both. Moreover, the absence of effective enforcement at the UN level leaves a great deal of scope for unilateral and collective resort to economic and military forms of coercion in which objectives are not necessarily defined in terms of community values, but rather in the light of special interests. It is certainly relevant to this inquiry to survey briefly some of the important developments in modern economic warfare. To some extent, it was its apparent success in two world wars which gave rise to widespread belief in the efficacy of economic measures as international sanctions.

9

TRADITIONAL SIEGE AND BLOCKADE TACTICS

Economic strength is a vital component of power and in the course of war it is an obvious target for attack, by military as well as by economic means. The traditional siege involved the combined use of military and economic pressure, and the development of sea power and naval warfare brought new opportunities for weakening the enemy's economic strength over a period of time. Not only could enemy ships be captured or destroyed; in an extension of siege tactics, a naval blockade of the enemy coast could be instituted to prevent shipping from calling at enemy ports to discharge or take on cargo. For a country heavily engaged in seaborne foreign trade, an interruption of foreign commerce could be an important factor in its powers of resistance. In addition to prohibiting trading with the enemy and destroying his shipping, belligerents claimed the right of visit and search of neutral ships on the high seas for contraband cargo, i.e., goods destined for enemy use and directly related to his war effort.

The Napoleonic Wars brought the first example of blockade on a significant scale and pointed to the future potentialities of economic warfare. It could not be claimed, however, that the Continental Blockade or the counter-measures adopted by Britain in the early years of the nineteenth century were in any way decisive in effect.[1] Inconvenience was suffered by all parties, but the belligerents were to a large extent self-sufficient in food and in the limited range of raw materials then necessary for the prosecution of war, and the armies of the day were unmechanized. The efforts of both sides in these blockades were not directed at paralysing war industries, but at bringing about commercial ruin and shortage of food by dislocating trade.

Throughout the nineteenth century, the variety of materials and products entering into international trade increased continuously and dramatically as a result of advances in technology, improvements in transport, discoveries of new sources of energy, and the acquisition of overseas empires. Colonization in particular added to the diversity and frequency of links between countries and between continents, and international commercial and capital transactions assumed major dimensions. Commerce was no longer a peripheral or marginal international activity; in many cases it had become necessary for the maintenance of industrial activity and national prosperity.

Increased participation in international trade and investment offered new scope and dimensions for economic warfare. Industrialized countries like Britain and Belgium became extremely vulnerable to interference with their imports of food and raw materials. In addition, by 1914, scientific discovery and technical progress had changed the character of war just as they had changed the character of economic life. Armies had become mechanized; many earlier combat techniques were obsolete. In the course of the First World War road transport began to supplement rail transport and tanks made their first appearance. Warships and submarines menaced the seas; weapons had become more complicated, more accurate, and more destructive; by the end of the war the importance of air warfare was becoming obvious. Access to minerals such as iron ore, petroleum, copper, manganese, nickel and other ferro-alloys, and to commodities such as rubber and cotton was vital for the maintenance of the war effort of an industrial power facing others of the same rank, and none could boast of complete self-sufficiency. The scope of war had been extended beyond the actual theatres of combat to affect the whole nation and every aspect of its people's lives, and even neutral states found it impossible to remain completely aloof and maintain normal patterns of economic life.

Nineteenth century rules governing blockade in international law became obsolete in the twentieth century. Distinctions between different categories of contraband were meaningless in conditions of total mobilization of resources for war, while the limitation of a blockade to the enemy's coastline and ports was unrealistic in an age of submarine and air warfare.

WORLD WAR 1914–1918

It is not surprising that the technique of economic warfare developed in the course of the First World War should be authoritatively described as "vastly different from anything that had been known before, with a new range of effectiveness".[2] For the Allied powers Germany's trade with neutral countries was an economic target of prime importance. At the same time the German submarine threat to British merchant shipping assumed serious dimensions, taking a heavy toll of imports and leading to shortages of food and other essential goods.

Britain's blockade of Germany was made official in March 1915 as a declared reprisal for submarine warfare. It covered all German trade, ignoring earlier distinctions between types of contraband. The hazards of inspection at sea, and the impossibility of maintaining a close blockade of the traditional type under conditions of modern naval warfare meant that new methods had to be devised to make the blockade effective. Examination of neutral shipping could be carried on in suitable 'control ports', but this led to considerable delays. In the interests of both Britain and the neutrals a system of navicerts was introduced. Navicerts were documents certifying neutral destination; they were issued at source and thus eliminated the need for further inspection of cargoes at sea.

Britain's blockade effort also included agreements with neutral governments and trade associations that they would not allow re-exports of goods to Germany or her allies – with continuation of trade with Britain as a *quid pro quo*; rationing of neutral importers to pre-war levels of trade; the 'blacklisting' of names of persons or concerns in neutral countries who were suspected of having – or were known to have – enemy connections and with whom dealings of any kind were consequently prohibited; and the refusal or threat of refusal of bunker and other port facilities to ships engaged in enemy trade. A wide ranging intelligence service proved essential, but the co-operation of exporters in neutral countries was of equal value. This was a new kind of blockade, enforced at long range through control of contraband and by agreement with neutrals, and bearing little resemblance to the old-style direct naval blockade of the enemy coast.

The United States insisted on the observance of its rights as a neutral in the early years of the war, objecting to such practices as bunker control and blacklisting on the grounds of serious inconvenience and infringement of sovereignty, but after it entered the war, it adopted all these practices, and co-operated with Britain in enforcing the blockade. The United States also made use of export control as a bargaining lever with neutrals.

The Allied blockade was undoubtedly a factor in Germany's eventual defeat. Shortages of essential materials such as copper, tin, rubber, and cotton became acute, particularly as Germany had not expected and was, therefore, inadequately prepared for a war lasting several years. The German government was driven to extreme lengths to conserve supplies of these materials and to develop artificial substitutes,[3] but lack of food may have been a more powerful factor in the German defeat than lack of raw materials. W. N. Medlicott considers that the effects of the blockade were exaggerated, particularly by German commentators, with the result that undue value was placed on economic pressure as a means of maintaining international peace.[4]

Blockade, as planned and executed by the British Ministry of Economic Warfare in the Second World War, formed part of a wider programme of unrestricted economic warfare which included the concentrated bombing of industrial targets in Germany. Control of German exports dated from November 1939 and was effective in reducing trade almost immediately.[5] Interception of German imports at sea was of much less significance than the controls exercised at source; air warfare, submarines, mines, radar, and other advances in technology made a long-distance blockade essential, the object being to prevent goods destined for the enemy from being shipped at all. The techniques devised in the First World War were developed and refined: compulsory navicerts were supplemented by ship warrants which were issued when the ship's owner agreed to comply with British regulations. Without this document no facilities were provided by or at British ports. Blacklisting was again extensively employed; pre-emptive buying of essential raw materials was undertaken when possible; neutrals were rationed for imports by means of a quota system. Britain had to exercise care in her negotiations with neutrals on whom she was dependent for certain imports; there was always the danger that if pressed too hard they would be driven into the Axis camp.

Co-operation with the United States was close after the latter entered the war. The US government's economic offensive relied heavily on the control of foreign funds and it also licensed exports to neutrals, instituted a proclaimed (black) list, and undertook pre-emptive buying of scarce items essential to the Axis war effort.

In this war Germany was less isolated than she had been in the previous conflict and could draw on supplies from a much larger area, particularly after she had overrun most of the continent of Europe and Italy had entered the war as an ally. Moreover, a self-sufficiency programme dating from the 1930s had encouraged the development of synthetics and substitutes and had built up stocks of goods in short supply. Partial evasion of the Allied blockade through neutral intermediaries was achieved throughout the war, but to a progressively smaller extent as a result of strenuous efforts by the Allies to control it. Wolfram from Spain and Portugal, ball-bearings from Sweden, and chrome ore from Turkey were not effectively denied to Germany until 1944.

In his authoritative study of the Allied blockade from 1939 to 1945, Medlicott notes that "the Ministry of Economic Warfare, in association with its American colleagues, had five main fields of achievement".

These were:

1. The drastic limitation of German imports from non-European sources, reduced after November 1942 to the small, desparate contribution of the blockade runners;

2. The creation of an encirclement neurosis with marked effect on German political and military strategy;

3. The direct hampering of the Axis armament effort by the creation of raw material shortages;

4. The indirect hampering of the Axis wartime economy by additional strains on transport and manpower;

5. The strengthening of neutral resistance to Axis pressure by economic aid, by the constant evidence of Allied determination, and by threats of retaliation, immediate or delayed.[6] But although the Allied effort in economic warfare undoubtedly had its effect in weakening Germany's war potential and capacity and contributed to her eventual defeat, it is not contended, or generally considered that it was a decisive factor at any stage.

The case of Japan was rather different. Lacking adjacent neutrals from whom she could draw supplies and, like Britain, vulnerable to interference with her shipping routes by air and sea attacks, she was seriously affected by traditional blockage tactics. In particular, shortages of minerals which resulted from the Allied blockage all but halted Japanese industries engaged in war production which were not, in any case, able to compete with Allied output.[7]

Blockade could play no part in a future world conflict involving nuclear weapons, but it can still be used in limited conflicts. To be effective, it must close air, as well as sea routes of supply. In 1948 the Western powers' air lift of supplies to West Berlin effectively overcame the 'blockade' imposed by the Soviet authorities who closed all road, rail and water links with the city; in the Nigerian civil war, the Biafrans were able to prolong their resistance as a result of arms and military equipment flown in from outside; Israel was supplied with military materiel by the US flown from Europe during the October 1973 war.

The experience of economic warfare built up largely as a result of the two major conflicts of this century is undoubtedly relevant to the process of international economic coercion but certain points should be borne in mind. Strong coalitions of states faced each other in both wars and no consideration of limiting the amount of damage inflicted on the enemy were operative. The undoubted achievements of the Allied effort in the economic sphere were produced in a situation of total war over a period of years; in the Second World War national survival was at stake; priorities were not in serious dispute; the forces and resources of the United States, Britain, and their allies were wholly committed to winning the war. It is obvious that any effort by the Security Council or the Assembly to discipline a recalcitrant state is likely to be qualitatively different; one cannot envisage an all-out UN effort in which economic measures would supplement military measures in a manner comparable to that of the 1939–45 war. If military conflict is to be avoided, even a blockade may be ruled out, particularly as an air blockade brings the danger of open conflict very close. Furthermore, as already noted, economic warfare, even in its most unrestricted and inhumane application, is not thought to have been a decisive factor in either world war.

Economic warfare of a more limited type also characterized the post-war years which produced the cold war between East and West, the formation of blocs and defensive alliances, policies of confrontation and recurring outbreaks of violence in various parts of the world. Economic measures of different kinds have been employed in some of these situations by states acting individually or in groups, on occasion in conjunction with military measures and often with no reference to, or authorization by, United Nations organs.

The past thirty-five years have also seen the extension and adaptation of the techniques of economic embargo and boycott.[8] Although the term 'boycott' dates only from the 1880s (when Captain Boycott became the first of many Irish landowners to suffer from organized refusal of social and commercial dealings) the practice of refusing to buy from, or sell to other merchants, or to have commercial relations with other political entities was well known in earlier times. Boycott expresses hostility or disapproval, but it may also represent an attempt to coerce recalcitrant groups or individuals in cases where the use of force is not contemplated, or feasible. In the form of blacklisting, as mentioned earlier, it has been applied by belligerents to firms in neutral states in time of war.

Originally boycott was a type of ostracism, a peaceful instrument of struggle, but today it is often virtually indistinguishable from other types of economic warfare organized under government auspices. Two programmes merit particular attention: Western strategic embargoes against communist countries and the Arab nations' economic war against Israel.

WESTERN STRATEGIC EMBARGOES IN EUROPE
AND THE FAR EAST

Controls over the export of strategic goods to the Soviet Union and East European Communist countries were instituted by the United States and its Western allies in 1948 as part of their cold war strategy. To facilitate multilateral co-operation in controlling trade with the Communist world all NATO countries (except Iceland) became informally associated in a Consultative Group (CG) in January 1950. Japan joined the group in 1952; Greece and Turkey in 1953. A standing Co-ordinating Committee (COCOM) was set up to implement policy decisions of the CG. There was no formal treaty basis for the CG–COCOM arrangements, although they were clearly an adjunct to NATO policy. Their organization, discussions, and activities were never publicized and even the names, "which indicate nothing whatsoever of the field of activity which is to be co-ordinated or consulted about . . . were considered to be classified material as late as 1953".[9]

In order to prevent the Soviet bloc from obtaining weapons or materials which would add to its military or economic potential, controls were placed on the export of a large number of items, set out in three international lists. Items on List I were subject to complete embargo; items on List II were subject to quantitative restrictions; List III contained items to be watched and on which information would be exchanged. These lists represented the minimum levels of control: individual countries could extend the lists if they wished.

The criteria determining inclusion of an item and its allocation to a particular list were the use of that item by Communist countries; its availability in the West; the availability of alternative sources of supply; the amount of technology contained in the item; the type of goods which might be received in exchange; and its strategic value.

Each country organized its own national system of control, using export licensing as the basic instrument, with supplementary controls over destination, transhipment, and transit of designated goods. The United Kingdom applied controls to munitions, atomic energy materials, and some industrial goods.

The United States formalized its control system through the Export Control Act (1949) and the Mutual Defense Assistance Control Act, (the Battle Act 1951) which prohibited trade in strategic goods with countries under Communist domination and provided for the withdrawal of United States aid from any country which knowingly shipped goods on the proscribed lists to Communist-controlled destinations. An absolute ban was imposed on arms, atomic energy materials, and military materiel; other items on a supplementary list, if shipped by third countries, might not produce the cessation of aid if the President of the United States considered that its continuance was important for his country's security.

The Consultative Group's embargoes and controls were first extended to cover Far Eastern trade during the Korean War, when the General Assembly recommended "additional economic measures" against Communist China and North Korea.[10] A second co-ordinating committee, CHINCOM, was set up in September 1952 to deal with exports to these areas, and a virtual embargo was imposed on all exports of industrial equipment and raw materials, with supplementary restraints on shipping and bunkering. North Vietnam was later added to the list of proscribed areas. Japan joined the CG and enforced restrictions of comparable severity.

As cold war tension tended to lessen in Europe during the 1950s, and it became obvious that Soviet technology was very highly advanced and not dependent upon imports of goods or know-how from the West, there was considerable pressure from the European participants in COCOM for a relaxation of the controls. In 1954 the US agreed that their scope should be narrowed and an item-by-item review of the international lists was undertaken: the number of items on List I was reduced from 260 to 170; and on List II from 90 to 20. The embargo on arms was not affected.

These relaxations, applied only to the Soviet Union and Soviet-oriented countries in Europe, but two years later, to the chagrin of the United States administration, Britain and Japan pressed hard for the elimination of the China differential: 207 items which could be sent to Eastern Europe but not to Communist China. The United States elected to maintain a full embargo on trade, shipping, and financial transactions with North Korea, North Vietnam, and Communist China but early in 1957 the other members of the Consultative Group abolished the China differential.

Further reductions in List I and the abolition of Lists II and III came in 1958 and in the 1960s the limitations of the programme came to be generally acknowledged, even in the United States.[11] Soviet military capacity was clearly not affected by embargoes and the progress of the Soviet economy was not being seriously hampered; moreover the US began to count the cost in domestic economic terms of limiting foreign trade for national security reasons. A further review of the COCOM list in 1965–66 brought in a system of administrative exceptions to the embargoes, whereby licences could be granted in special circumstances and reported to COCOM, and differences in treatment of individual East European countries were confirmed. Yugoslavia, which had been treated as a western country since 1956, joined GATT in 1966; Poland, Romania and Hungary had all joined by 1973. The US itself had serious balance of payment problems and was looking for increased trade opportunities, and in the early 1970s an expansion of commercial relations between the US and the USSR and Eastern Europe became an important part of the overall policy of detente pursued by the Nixon and Ford Administrations.

In contrast to the 1967 Trade Expansion Act which gave the prevention of communist economic penetration as one of the stated purposes of multilateral trade negotiations, the 1974 Trade Act emphasised expansion of US trade through trade agreements with non-market (Socialist) economies as well as with other industrial economies and less developed countries.[12]

The position at the time of writing is that there are no restrictions on the export of 'peaceful goods' (except those in short supply) to the USSR, Eastern Europe or China. Licences are still needed for items on the COCOM list which is maintained by the US and its western allies. Grzybowski describes these items as a "highly selective group of advanced technology equipment and material that exhibits dual pattern uses for both civilian and military applications".[13] Military materiel cannot be exported to these countries.

China

The case of China is particularly interesting. Although a General Assembly Resolution of 18 May 1951 recommended additional measures of an economic nature against both China and North Korea during the Korean war, the embargoes against China were largely a US initiative. Until the early 1970s, successive US administrations reinforced their policy of economic ostracism by refusing to recognize the Peking government as the government of China and by supporting the Nationalist government of Taiwan both inside and outside the UN where it occupied the 'China' seat. Doubts about the value of the US embargo policy in practical terms were voiced by the Congressional Joint Economic Committee as early as 1967; it noted that "an overwhelming consensus among the experts heard by the Committee" pointed to the conclusions that the embargo on non-strategic trade with China had accomplished very little in terms of retarding growth of the Chinese economy, and might actually have been detrimental to the long run interests of the United States.[14] Some relaxation of control over non-commercial importation of Chinese goods into the US and over trade with China by US subsidiaries abroad came in 1969, but the seating of PRC representatives in the UN in 1971 and President Nixon's visit to Peking in February 1972 ushered in a new period of US-China relations. Controls on many non-strategic items were lifted, China and the USSR were classified equally and trade between the US and China expanded rapidly. The hostility of the years between 1949 and 1971 became a thing of the past.

From the point of view of this study, the interesting aspects of the Chinese case are not only the demonstrated sterility and futility of the US position of non-recognition and economic ostracism, but also the extent to which China twice re-oriented its foreign trade to meet altered external circumstances.

In the years prior to the Communist revolution of 1949–50, China's trade was chiefly conducted outside the Soviet bloc. Seventy-four per cent of her foreign trade was with non-Communist countries and only 26 per cent with the Communist world, of which 23 per cent was trade with the Soviet Union.

Under Western embargoes, and while closely allied with the Soviet bloc, trade patterns altered. Between 1952 and 1959, 57 to 60 per cent of China's exports went to Eastern Europe and the Soviet Union, and 55 to 79 per cent of imports originated from there.

China received complete plant installations, military materiel, industrial raw materials, and technical assistance from the Soviet bloc. Her gross national product grew at an average rate of 8 per cent per annum but at the price of considerable economic dependence on the rest of the Communist world. By 1960 bloc trade constituted 66 per cent of China's total imports and exports: a complete reversal of the picture a decade earlier.

The rift with the Soviet Union led to a cessation of Soviet aid in 1960. Technicians were withdrawn, aid agreements cancelled, exports and credits summarily cut off. The Chinese were forced to initiate a second re-orientation of their external trade. One of their first projects was to reduce dependence on supplies of petroleum from the Soviet Union. An intensive local programme of exploration and extraction was followed by orders for refining equipment from Western firms in 1964–5. Outstanding debts to the Soviet Union were also paid off by 1965. The stimulation of domestic agricultural production to reduce dependence on imported food supplies was reflected in heavy imports of artificial fertilizers. By 1965 the Communist world was responsible for only 32 per cent of China's imports and took 27 per cent of her exports. Hong Kong had supplanted the Soviet Union as the main export market, taking 20 per cent of all Chinese exports. Australia, Canada, and Japan became major suppliers of imports to China, Canadian wheat being particularly important. Eckstein points out that by the late 1960s, "the trade pattern was totally reversed, China's trade with Communist countries encompassing 20 to 25 per cent and with non-Communist countries 75 to 80 per cent of the total".[15]

The effects of the Western embargoes are hard to judge but it is clear that they outlived their usefulness. Wolf, in a thoughtful analysis, suggests that the original policy was based on some erroneous assumptions and became entrenched.[16] Clearly, as the 'bipolar world' vanished the economic warfare seen as appropriate to contain communism became increasingly irrelevant; a far more complex set of international political and economic relationships had to be handled. And the US itself became vulnerable to pressure as the Arab oil embargo was to show.

ARAB BOYCOTTS AND EMBARGOES

The primary target of Arab economic pressure has been Israel, although secondary boycotts and embargoes have been applied to organizations and companies in third countries which have close economic ties with Israel or which appear to be contributing to Israeli military capacity. The Arab boycott, which amounts to a programme of economic 'cold' warfare has been sponsored by the League of Arab States, a regional organization registered under Chapter VIII of the UN Charter.

Members of the Arab League challenged the existence of Israel from the moment it became a state and joined the UN in 1948. Boycott resolutions date from 1945 but in 1951, the Council of the League gave the boycott a more formal character;[17] a central Boycott Office in Damascus, headed by a Commissioner-General, was established to direct the campaign and co-ordinate the activities of regional boycott offices which are located in each member state. The boycott imposed a total ban on all Arab dealings with Israel of a commercial or personal nature; in addition, all trade agreements between Arab and other countries were required to contain a clause forbidding the re-export of Arab products to Israel, and of Israeli products, whether processed or not, to Arab states.

Israeli shipping was banned from Arab ports and Israeli aircraft denied landing and overflight privileges by Arab countries. The severance of communication was carried to the point that no ship, of whatever registration, could call at an Arab port in the course of a voyage during which it had also called at an Israeli port, and no aircraft could fly over, or land in, Arab territory if it had previously landed in Israel. Egypt closed the Suez Canal to Israeli ships, and to other ships carrying cargo to or from Israel, as early as May 1948, and the restrictions were maintained until after the 1973 war in spite of Security Council resolutions calling for their termination. The Arab countries have also employed the technique of blacklisting to widen the scope of their campaign. A secondary boycott covers Arab trade with foreign firms who have close Israeli connections in the form of subsidiary companies, factories, or plants in Israel, or who give technical assistance to Israeli industries. Such firms must sever their links with Israel or submit to the boycott themselves. As a counter-inducement, assistance has been offered to firms which move their factories from Israel to any Arab state.

It is public knowledge that Western-owned companies have been obliged to forgo planned dealings with, or investment in Israel under threat of extension of the Arab boycott to them. For instance, from 1957 to 1959 Air France was blacklisted because of a planned plane-lease agreement with El Al and reported investment in the Israeli film industry; two years later the Renault company was threatened with a boycott of its products throughout the Arab world if it proceeded with plans to establish an assembly plant in Israel.[18] A threatened boycott of the British insurance firm, Norwich Union led to the resignation of Lord Mancroft, a Jewish director; adverse reaction brought an official statement from the Secretary of the Arab League that the boycott was "protective and defensive": Arab countries objected to firms having commercial relations with Israel only if they strengthened Israel's economy, its war effort, and expansionist, aggressive intentions.[19] Obviously criteria are applied subjectively on a case-by-case basis.

Early in 1965 Imperial Chemical Industries and its seventy-seven subsidiary companies were boycotted for three months because of alleged dealings with Israel, while in November 1966, at the 24th Conference of the Regional Boycott Bureaux, a unanimous decision was taken to blacklist the three American corporations, Radio Corporation of America (RCA), Ford, and Coca Cola.[20] In the mid-1970s further publicity was given to Arab blacklisting; Sony and Leyland were offered exemption from the list if they would cancel contracts with Israel.[21]

An office set up by the Israeli government in 1960 to organize counter-boycott measures was closed in 1971 because the boycott was seen as ineffective, but the events of the 1970s revealed this judgement to be ill-founded. The growing wealth of many Arab countries enhanced their attractions as trading partners and a new Israeli anti-boycott unit was established in September 1975 to co-ordinate efforts to expose the discriminatory effects of the primary and secondary boycott.[22] In this, it has had some success.

In 1977, the US Export Administration Amendment Act attempted to restrict the effect of the Arab boycott by providing the President with powers to prohibit any US national from complying with a "boycott fostered or imposed by a foreign country against a country which is friendly to the United States" and which is not itself under boycott by the US.[23] 'Compliance' in terms of the Act covers refusal to do business with the target of the boycott at the behest of the boycotters, and also such acts as supplying information to the boycotters about business relationships and involvement in charitable organizations and shipping transactions with the boycotted country.

Other governments have also taken anti-boycott measures; for instance in 1976 the Canadian government withdrew government financing and insurance assistance from companies complying with the Arab boycott of Israel and legislation requiring companies to report Arab requests for boycott clauses has been proposed; such clauses would clearly be illegal under the US legislation, as they are under a provincial law in Ontario.

But the limitations of these anti-boycott measures are obvious. The US itself has imposed boycotts, viewing them as an acceptable foreign policy instrument, and has, on occasions, exerted pressure on third parties to support them, for instance against Cuba; moreover a major concern behind the 1974 legislation was to restrict intervention in US domestic affairs.[24] The legislation also includes a clause establishing that "the mere absence of a business relationship with or in the boycotted country . . . does not indicate the existance of the intent required to establish a violation . . ." The subtle effect of the Arab boycott can thus be to prevent business relationships being established with Israel and this is hard to counter.

A prime effect of the Arab boycott has been to deprive Israel of oil from the Middle East which could have been brought by pipeline. It has also been a hindrance to foreign companies and business interests forced to choose between two profitable markets instead of making investments or instituting trading links with both. More seriously, the economic isolation of Israel from normal commerce with its neighbours has obviously been detrimental to all parties through loss of convenient markets, sources of supply, cooperation in transportation, schemes for natural resources development and tourism.[25] But recurring, if short-lived wars, and continuing guerrilla activity and Israeli reprisals, plus the civil war in Lebanon, have compounded these effects and placed heavy strains on the economies of Israel, Egypt, Syria and Jordan. Defence accounts for an increasing proportion of their budgets and they become increasingly dependent on external sources for military equipment and financial support. The peace treaty between Israel and Egypt signed in March 1979 signalled the end of economic warfare between them and both countries should benefit. But it is too soon to judge the impact of the Arab boycott of Egypt adopted in retaliation for Egypt's 'defection' from the anti-Israel front.

The Oil Weapon

The enormous oil resources of Saudi Arabia and the Gulf States are so important to western economies that it was probably inevitable that use of the oil weapon would be expanded in the Arabs' economic war against Israel. In the summer of 1967 following the Six-Day Middle East War, there were proposals from the Arab Central Boycott office for stringent measures against the US, Britain and West Germany in retaliation for their alleged support of Israeli 'aggression'. Recommendations for general embargoes on exports and imports and nationalization of oil installations were not approved; a short-lived ban on oil supplies was lifted at the end of August as it was proving ineffective and costly. Western countries were able to import oil from other sources and their economies were not seriously affected.

But things were to be quite different in 1973 when the oil embargo captured world headlines and subjected the major western powers and Japan to shortages and the prospect of economic disaster. The dangers of the heavy and increasing dependence by western industrialized countries on imported oil, were already apparent. And a new solidarity among oil producers was demonstrated in Teheran in 1971 when OPEC insisted on a major price rise and an increased share in the oil companies' assets and profits. Warnings from Saudi Arabia that the oil weapon would be used if the US continued to give Israel military support preceded the events of October 1973 when cutbacks of production by the OAPEC group of oil producers, total embargoes on supplies to the US and the Netherlands, and linking of continued supplies to the adoption of a pro-Arab stance by other importing states confronted a badly organized group of consumer countries with some hard choices. Neither alternative supplies of oil nor alternative sources of energy were readily available.

Petroleum has long been recognized as the prime strategic commodity through which economic leverage can be applied.[26] It is the world's major energy resource, is indispensable for civilian and military road and air transportation and is also a vital raw material for the chemical industry. New sources of supply have come into production (in Alaska, Nigeria, the North Sea) and others are exploitable (the continental shelf of China, Vietnam; the Athabasca tar sands). There is also research and development into alternative sources of energy, such as nuclear power and solar energy. But some of these are limited in quantity, others need a very high price for energy to make them profitable, all will take time to develop. There are also environmental concerns about the use of nuclear power. For the immediate future, oil imports are vital to Western Europe and Japan and increasingly important to the US. In 1973 Japan imported approximately 90 per cent of its energy requirements; oil accounted for 79 per cent of these requirements and virtually all was imported, 80 per cent from Middle East sources. In the same year, Western Europe imported 62 per cent of its energy needs, of which nearly all was oil from the Middle East.[27] The US is less dependent on imported energy but its level of imports is increasing. Oil accounted for 46 per cent of US energy consumption in 1974 and 63 per cent was domestically produced. Of the 37 per cent imported, 12.3 per cent came from Arab OPEC members.[28]

A brief chronology of the use of the oil weapon may be helpful here.[29] War between Israel and the Arabs began on 6 October 1973, with the Egyptian attack on the Sinai; on 17 October at an emergency meeting of Arab oil ministers in Kuwait (Abu-Dhabi, Algeria, Bahrain, Egypt, Iraq, Kuwait, Libya, Qatar, Saudi-Arabia, Syria) it was decided that oil production would be reduced each month by at least 5 per cent from the September 1973 level until all Israeli forces were evacuated from territory occupied in the 1967 war and the legitimate rights of the Palestinians were restored, but that supplies of oil to countries friendly to the Arabs would not suffer. Action by individual Arab producers implemented this decision. A cease-fire was finally established on the Suez and Syrian fronts on 24 October but the oil weapon was not shelved. On 4–5 November the oil ministers met again in Kuwait and decided to make the initial production cut 25 per cent of the September level and a further 5 per cent for each succeeding month. The 25 per cent cut was to include the complete embargo of oil shipments to the US and the Netherlands and any other country supporting Israel.

A letter from OAPEC to the American people published in the *Washington Post* of 14 November 1973, and an advertisement placed in the *Guardian* on 15 November stressed the objectives of liberating the occupied territories and restoring the rights of the Palestinians; and promising that friendly countries would continue to receive the same amount of oil supply as before. Reference was also made to the precedent set by US strategic embargoes.

At an Arab Summit Conference held in Algiers from 26–28 November and attended by the leaders of 16 countries (excluding

Iraq and Libya) it was resolved that use of the oil weapon would continue. A committee was to be charged with the duty of drawing up a list classifying countries as 'friendly', 'neutral' and 'supporting the enemy'. This list was to be reviewed periodically and countries reclassified in the light of their "commitment to implement the political line decided upon by the Arab summit . . ." The exemption of Japan and the Philippines from the December cutbacks and a total embargo on Portugal, Rhodesia and South Africa were also agreed upon.

By December 8, when the Arab oil ministers met again in Kuwait, shifts in position by the EEC countries (except the Netherlands) brought the suspension of the 5 per cent reduction of their oil imports and Saudi Arabia postponed its December production cut-back. The prospect of raising the embargo on supplies to the US was noted, provided agreement was reached on Israeli withdrawal from Jerusalem and the occupied territories. In fact, the embargo on the US was lifted by all Arab governments except Libya and Iraq on March 18, 1974, without the fulfilment of these conditions. At the same meeting Italy and West Germany were classified as 'friendly'. The ban on exports to the Netherlands was not raised until July, while the ban on South Africa remained in effect. South Africa, like Israel, has imported most of its oil requirements from Iran, but while Israel has an agreement with the US whereby it is promised oil from US sources if traditional external supplies are cut off, South Africa has no such protection. Its vulnerability to an oil embargo is discussed further in Chapter 7 below.

The economic effects of the Arab cutbacks and embargoes were felt by *all* importers of petroleum and petroleum products, mainly as a result of the five-fold rise in prices which they clearly accelerated.[30] Between October 1973 and January 1974, the posted price of Persian Gulf crude oil rose from $2.30 per barrel to $11.65 per barrel. Definitive statements about the economic effect of the embargo on the United States or other importers are not possible; it appears that Libya and Iraq did not cut production and that oil from these sources and from Abu-Dhabi reached the US via the Caribbean.[31]

But if the economic effects of the boycott are hard to separate from the effects of soaring prices, the political effects are hardly in dispute. In Japan and Western Europe there was consternation and an obvious swing to a markedly pro-Arab stance. In December 1973, the Deputy Premier of Japan visited eight Arab states; Egypt was offered a 25 year loan of $140 million for improvement of the Suez Canal, as well as Japanese assistance for other development projects. Western European governments were not far behind in pledging friendship and offering bilateral trade agreements, technology, arms deals and general economic assistance to Arab governments. *Sauve qui peut* unilateralism was very much to the fore during the late autumn and early winter months and the refusal of European members of NATO (except Portugal) to co-operate in the US airlift of equipment to Israel during the October war strained relations within the alliance. Clearly, the Arabs had maintained solidarity in pursuit of the goal of swinging Western governments to their side and had thereby increased Israel's isolation. The fact that third world countries were to sustain a heavy additional burden on their balance of payments as a result of the oil price rises, did not affect their pro-Arab and pro-Palestinian stance, and the communist countries were also opposed to Israel. This left the US as Israel's only powerful friend. Subsequent developments revealed American anxiety to develop and maintain good relations with both Israel and the Arab countries and its willingness to exert strong pressure on Israel to conclude a peace treaty with Egypt.

When the embargo was first imposed, there was a sharp reaction in the US. Secretary of State Kissinger spoke of blackmail and the possible use of force[32] and there was discussion of possible counter-embargoes. A feasibility study of a US food embargo was prepared for the House Committee on Foreign Affairs in November 1973.[33] But generally, the US accepted the embargo without direct retaliation. If it had been prolonged, or more effective against the US, this might not have been the case. Both President Ford and Mr. Carter (as Presidential candidate) when asked about their reaction to any future oil embargo stated that they would not tolerate it. Mr. Carter said he would treat it as an economic declaration of war and would respond instantly and in kind.[34]

Concern about future embargoes prompted a Congressional Committee study of the feasibility of US military occupation of foreign oil fields.[35] This report noted that "sustained sanctions by the Arab States, perhaps abetted by Iran, would disrupt this country domestically and degrade US security but not even a full scale OPEC embargo would threaten US survival . . . Energy shortages averaging 10–15 per cent could be tolerated until permanent adjustments were made." On the other hand "serious oil

embargoes would shatter Western Europe and Japan . . ." and
"severe sanctions by oil-producing countries would thus involve
vital interests at a very early stage . . ."[36]

The West has also made progress in preparing contingency plans:
the International Energy Agency, set up as an adjunct to OECD in
November 1974, provides for the sharing of supplies among
members in a future emergency.[37]

Interdependence between the major Arab producers and the US
and heavy Arab investment in the western world have made a
future embargo on the Pan-Arab scale less likely. Economic
depression and collapse in the west can hardly serve Arab interests.
But shortages resulting from internal upheaval, such as in Iran in
early 1979, underline the strategic nature of the resource, and
threats of embargo may be effective in maintaining pro-Arab
attitudes among major importers.[38]

The Arab governments vehemently denied that the measures
they employed were a form of blackmail or a threat to peace; they
claimed that they were exercising their sovereign rights over their
natural resources, that the production cutbacks were in the interests
of conservation, while the selective embargoes were designed only to
penalize countries which were helping Israel to retain Arab lands
and blocking the legitimate rights of self-determination of the
Palestinian people. Arab spokesmen denied that economic coercion
has become illegal either through the UN Charter or interpretations
thereof in General Assembly resolutions provided it is being used to
counter the military strength of a hostile power; in such circumstances, and in the absence of any internationally enforced
protection of the militarily weaker state, it becomes a form of self
defence.[39]

No government, except the Israeli government, actually challenged the Arabs' use of the oil weapon on legal grounds. It might have
been awkward for the United States to do so, given its own record of
discriminatory export controls, although governments do not
necessarily, or usually, refrain from accusing others of violating laws
which they have not themselves been scrupulous in observing. One
has to conclude that among oil consumers discretion was the
guiding principle and conciliation rather than aggravation the
primary response. In other words, economic pressure worked.

3 Regional Sanctioning Programmes

Western embargoes on trade with Communist countries in Europe and the Far East, like Arab boycotts and embargoes have been the product of war or of near-war situations. The objective is to strengthen one's own position, weaken the enemy, and prevent the development of his military and industrial strength.

The Soviet-sponsored boycotts of Yugoslavia and Albania, and the United States action against Cuba supported by the OAS, fall in a somewhat different category. Action in these cases was inspired by the perceived defection of one member of the regional grouping, posing a threat to the internal stability and security of the region. Economic sanctions were imposed in an attempt to bring a return to conformity.

SOVIET AND EAST EUROPEAN BOYCOTTS

Yugoslavia

In 1948 the Soviet Union and the East European countries, acting through the Cominform, expelled Yugoslavia from the bloc and instituted a programme of ostracism. Diplomatic relations were severed, economic links cut and a propaganda campaign designed to discredit the Yugoslav government under Marshal Tito went into full strength. Trade ceased, debts were not settled, borders were sealed.[1]

The occasion for this concentrated programme of deprivation and calumny was the widening rift between Tito's government and the rest of the Communist bloc; unlike the other satellites, Yugoslavia had been developing an independent policy and refused to adhere uncritically to the official Stalinist line or to accept policy dictated from Moscow. As a result of the break with Eastern

Europe, Yugoslav policy had to undergo a fundamental reorientation and seek a more independent base. Politically, the Tito government developed its own brand of Communism and in foreign relations pursued a policy of non-alignment between East and West.

By mid-1949 virtually all economic relations between Yugoslavia and the rest of Eastern Europe had been severed. This general embargo constituted a severe blow to the Yugoslav economy which was still in process of recovering from the devastation and damage of the Second World War. The first Five-Year Plan for development (1947–51) aimed to double the national income (1939 level) and there was heavy emphasis on the expansion of industrial capacity and production. The Soviet Union and other East European countries had been prepared to supply capital goods on easy credit terms, in addition to giving aid and technical assistance. Joint Yugoslav-Soviet air and shipping companies had been set up. About one half of Yugoslavia's external trade had been conducted with the Communist bloc: in return for exports of raw materials and food, she imported fuel, processed goods, industrial materials, and rolling stock. The Soviet-orchestrated boycott meant the severance of co-operation in all fields and a drastic reorientation of trade, which could only be towards Western Europe. In 1948 Yugoslav imports from, and exports to, Western Europe were negligible: by 1952, as a result of the enforced shift in trade, 19.3 per cent of imports came from the United States and 20.3 per cent from West Germany, while 14.7 per cent of exports went to the former and 23.7 per cent to the latter. The character of foreign trade also changed somewhat over this period. Machinery was imported, and as secondary industry developed, manufactured goods bulked larger in exports until they became the third most important source of export earnings. This achievement was not made without hardship, or without incurring indebtedness to the West: between 1950 and 1954, one billion dollars of aid was granted to Yugoslavia.[2]

Although there were initial difficulties of negotiation due to resentment at Yugoslav expropriation of Western assets, the Export-Import Bank of the United States and the International Bank for Reconstruction and Development were providing loans by 1949. When, a year later, there was a severe crisis in Yugoslavia because of drought, the United States, France, and Britain organized tripartite aid, which continued until 1958.

The rapprochement between Yugoslavia and the Soviet Union which came in 1955 led to a 'normalization' of economic relations with Eastern Europe which was obviously to Yugoslavia's advantage. Long-term credits were again offered by the Soviet government and barter agreements led to a gradual increase in trade. Yugoslavia has participated in COMECON on a qualified basis since 1965, but Soviet-Yugoslav relations have never been cordial. In a study of the Yugoslav economy Ian Hamilton noted that, after a break with Cominform, the United States became and remained a "major source of fuel and machinery for Yugoslavia and a major market for Yugoslav non-ferrous metals and luxuries".[3]

Yugoslavia has continued to face economic problems, but a measure of economic independence has been achieved through cooperation with both East and West.

Political survival proved possible after 1948 in spite of severe external pressure; the force of national feeling was demonstrated and the leadership of Marshal Tito was strengthened. Practical assistance from the West tided the Yugoslav economy over the worst period, and in this instance the Soviet Union evidently judged it unwise to resort to force.

Albania

Albania's 'defection' to the Chinese Communist camp in 1961 led to the institution of a comparable, though less comprehensive, programme of denial by the Soviet Union and other East European countries. It could not be termed a full-scale boycott, for although most COMECON countries participated, both Poland and Czechoslovakia increased their trade with Albania between 1961 and 1962, and Poland concluded a trade agreement with Albania in 1962 which provided for the delivery of Polish machinery and rolling stock.

Albania was hard hit by the Soviet-sponsored action which took the familiar form of the suspension of credits, cancellation of technical assistance agreements, withdrawal of experts, the return of Albanian students and trainees from COMECON countries, and a very sharp reduction in trade, particularly with the USSR.[4] The Soviet Union had financed two Albanian Five-Year Plans (1951–5 and 1956–60) and had for years made up her chronic external deficit. Fifty per cent of Albania's total external trade was conducted with the Soviet Union prior to the breach, and dependence on imports of food is illustrated by the fact that in 1959 supplies of Soviet wheat equalled Albanian domestic production. There was a Soviet commitment to supply equipment and specialists for more than one hundred factories at the time when the boycott was imposed.

The boycott necessitated a reorientation, and if possible a reduction of external dependence. Relations with Communist China were already ideologically close and a groundwork of economic links existed which could be greatly extended, Communist China was Albania's most important non-COMECON trading partner as early as 1956.

Agreements signed between China and Albania in January 1962 provided for increased trade between the two countries. Canadian wheat purchased by China was shipped to Albania and the agreements provided for Chinese credits and technical assistance for the third Five-Year Plan (1961–5); the export of Chinese grain, steel, tractors, fertilizers, and other commodities in exchange for copper (first mined in Albania in 1961), chrome ore, petroleum, and tobacco. Chinese exports to Albania in 1962 equalled Soviet exports in 1960; by 1963 Sino-Albanian trade was five and half times its 1960 value. A Sino-Albanian shipping company was also established in 1962.

Albania ceased to subscribe to COMECON or to send representatives to its meetings in 1962. Instead, she sought to develop trade relations with the non-Communist world, and with neighbouring Yugoslavia.

Despite the COMECON boycott, Albania's growth rate increased considerably during the 1960s, surpassing planners' expectations. A loan from China helped to support the economy during the fourth Five-Year Plan (1966–70), but domestic sources came to provide an increasing proportion of funds for investment. But in the 1970s Sino-Albanian relations came to repeat the pattern of Soviet-Albanian relations; Albania accused China of collaboration with American imperialism and of aspirations to become a superpower and in 1978 China cut off all economic and military aid.

It remains to be seen whether Albania can survive without a major external source of aid and protection. Neither the US nor the USSR appear to be acceptable in this role and the diversification of economic links with Eastern European countries, Cuba and possibly Vietnam, are not a substitute. Albania is also vulnerable to Soviet pressure now that Chinese protection has been removed.

OAS SANCTIONS IN THE WESTERN HEMISPHERE

Action by the Organization of American States (OAS) is particularly interesting because of the organization's status as a well-developed regional system within the UN framework. It has sought, rather perfunctorily, to associate the UN with its sanctioning activities both against the Dominican Republic and against Cuba.

Dominican Republic

Economic sanctions were first invoked by the OAS in August 1960 when the Foreign Ministers of member states meeting at San José, Costa Rica, condemned the Trujillo regime in the Dominican Republic for committing acts of aggression and intervention in Venezuela and for its implication in the attempted assassination of the Venezuelan president.

Acting in terms of Articles 6 and 8 of the Rio Treaty, the Foreign Ministers passed a unanimous resolution which called for the breaking of diplomatic relations between all members of the OAS and the delinquent regime, the partial interruption of economic relations, and the immediate suspension of trade in arms and implements of war of every kind. The extension of embargoes to cover trade in other articles was to be studied, and the Security Council informed of OAS action. It was agreed that the measures would be discontinued when the government of the Dominican Republic ceased to constitute a danger to the peace and security of the hemisphere.

There was a division of opinion in the Security Council as to whether the OAS had acted improperly in not seeking prior authorization for its action, a point of view supported by the Soviet Union but opposed by the United States. The matter was left unresolved; the Security Council merely acknowledged receipt of the information from the Secretary-General of the OAS and noted the application of sanctions on a regional basis. The Soviet Union and Poland abstained from voting.

In January 1961 the Council of the OAS voted fourteen to one, with six abstentions, that it would be feasible to extend the embargo to include trade in petroleum and petroleum products, trucks and spare parts. Cuba voted in favour. The United States penalized imports of sugar from the Dominican Republic by imposing an entry fee of two cents a pound, payable in advance, and later prohibited the distribution to the Dominican Republic of part of the former Cuban quota.

In the course of 1961 Trujillo was assassinated and a more democratic regime installed. The political situation remained tense and US warships were stationed off the Dominican coast in November and December. The OAS sanctions were removed in January 1962 and the United States immediately extended an emergency credit of $25 million.[5]

The Dominican Republic as the small client of a super-power, with no outside support, offered the elements of a classic case for the application of external economic pressure. It is a leading supplier of sugar; nine-tenths of the crop is exported, and although coffee and cocoa are important exports, sugar accounts for over 50 per cent of the total value of exports. But the period in which sanctions were operating was too short to isolate their economic effects, and in any case the embargoes were limited in scope and not wholly observed. Some effects on trade can be discerned. Exports of unrefined sugar which were worth $80.1 million in 1960 were only $59.8 million in 1961; by 1963 they had recovered to $88.8 million.[6] Schreiber notes that the "primary economic effect of US sugar restrictions had been to prevent a large increase in Dominican revenues at a time when this could have substantially bolstered the troubled economy".[7]

Politically the effects of concerted condemnation and pressure by twenty nations in the hemisphere may have assisted internal resistance and helped to bring the downfall of Trujillo and his regime. More important, perhaps, was the accompaniment of economic coercion by military threats and intensive diplomatic pressure from the US, alongside CIA involvement in Dominican politics. The absence of any ideological alignments and the general unpopularity of the regime inside and outside the Dominican Republic simplified the issues in this case.[8]

It may be noted that the later course of United States relations with the Dominican Republic was far from smooth. Initially American military intervention in the Dominican Republic in 1965 was not undertaken with the support of the OAS, and was strongly opposed by a number of Latin American countries, particularly Chile, Ecuador, Mexico, Peru, and Uruguay.[9]

Cuba

The case of Cuba was more complicated and sanctions were more prolonged. Embargoes imposed unilaterally by the United States date from August 1960 – less than a year after Fidel Castro came to power in Cuba – and by October all United States exports were banned (with the exception of medicine and food) and the sugar quota had been reduced to zero. Diplomatic relations were severed in January 1961. These embargoes followed Cuban expropriation without compensation of American property valued by US Department of Commerce at $1,000 million and the imposition of discriminatory taxes and licences on American products.

All trade between the United States and Cuba (except medicine and food) was finally embargoed early in 1962, and the sale, charter, and transfer of ships to the Cuban government and its nationals were prohibited without official approval. Normal communication links by sea and air were also severed although an airlift of Cuban refugees continued. In the interim, however, there had been the abortive Bay of Pigs invasion and recourse to the OAS for support for United States action.

The United States had tried to raise the Cuban issue at the OAS meeting at San José in August in 1960, but was unable to obtain more than a general declaration rejecting any extra-continental intervention in Latin America and attempts by Sino-Soviet powers to make use of the political, economic or social situation in any American State.[10] During 1961, however, Castro publicly acknowledged his Marxist-Leninist affiliation and spoke of the Cuban revolution as a socialist, anti-imperialist movement. This posture enabled the United States to achieve stronger OAS support. At the 8th meeting of the OAS Organ of Consultation held at Punta Del Este in January 1962, adherence by any member of the OAS to Marxist-Leninist ideology was declared to be incompatible with the inter-American system. Only Cuba voted against the resolution. There being no provision for expulsion of members in the Bogota Charter, Cuba was declared to have placed herself 'voluntarily' outside the system (by a bare two-thirds majority of votes) and it was also resolved to suspend immediately trade with Cuba in arms and implements of war of every kind (16 votes in favour and 4 abstentions). The feasibility and desirability of extending the suspension of trade to other items, particularly those of strategic importance, were to be studied.

Cuba took her case to the Security Council and in March 1962 proposed that an Advisory Opinion should be sought from the International Court of Justice on questions relating to sanctions, claiming that the OAS measures should be suspended in the meantime. This suggestion was not taken up. In the Security Council debate, the United States asserted the OAS right to take any action without being hampered by the veto.

The development of the missile crisis in October 1962 brought a temporary unanimity in the OAS on the dangers of Castro's alignment with the Soviet Union. The United States was able to obtain unanimous OAS support on 23 October for enforcement of the 'quarantine' she had announced the previous day to prevent delivery of weapons to Cuba. A resolution passed by the OAS council, acting provisionally as the Organ of Consultation under the Rio Treaty, authorized members to take all measures individually and collectively, including the use of armed force, to ensure hemispheric security. Although the United States took the major responsibility for the blockade against the shipment of offensive weapons to Cuba, other OAS members offered or contributed ships, bases, and troops in support. The Security Council considered the matter on the same day, at the request of both the United States and Cuban governments, but took no action. The matter was settled directly between the United States and the Soviet Union; the quarantine, effective from 24 October, was lifted on 20 November.

The discovery of an arms cache in Venezuela early in 1964 led to further accusations of Cuban subversion; in July, at the 9th meeting of the Organ of Consultation of the OAS, both Venezuela and the United States called for mandatory sanctions. An OAS investigating committee had confirmed the Cuban origin of the arms found in the cache. Action was taken in accordance with the relevant articles of the Rio Treaty: all diplomatic relations were to be severed; all trade except food, medicine, and medical equipment was to be banned; no sea transport was to be permitted except for humanitarian reasons. Cuba was warned that persistence in 'aggression' might lead to resort to force in self defence. Chile, Bolivia, and Uruguay dissented from these recommendations, and Mexico did not comply with the decision to sever diplomatic relations.

In the meantime the United States continued its unilateral pressure on Cuba. In July 1963 all Cuban assets in United States banks had been frozen and all transactions concerning property with a Cuban interest had been placed under licence. The United

States government also sought support from its NATO allies for action against Cuba, though this attempt was not wholly successful. Canada's reaction was typical of the rest; embargoes were placed on strategic items which would contribute to Cuba's military strength, but normal trade continued.

The official aims of United States policy towards Cuba were set out by the then Under Secretary of State, George Ball, on 23 April 1964. Stating that "economic denial is a weapon that must be used with great selectivity. It can never be more effective than the economic circumstances of the target country", Mr. Ball indicated that the purpose of the programme was not to bring down the Castro regime, which would call for a blockade, but to accomplish four more limited objectives:

First, to reduce the will and ability of the present Cuban regime to export subversion and violence to the other American states;

Second, to make plain to the people of Cuba and to elements of the power structure of the regime that the present regime cannot serve their interests;

Third, to demonstrate to the people of the American Republics that communism has no future in the Western Hemisphere; and

Fourth, to increase the cost of maintaining a Communist outpost in the Western Hemisphere.[11]

He described the United States policy as the only policy, short of the use of force, which gave promise of having a significant impact on Cuba and its continuance as a Communist base in the Western hemisphere.

Although the success of United States policy in terms of the first three objectives is open to question, (as indeed is the propriety of the second objective), there can be no denying the heavy cost to the Soviet Union which the embargoes on Cuba have represented. Between 1960 and 1970 Soviet aid was of the order of $3.6 billion and Cuba also received $800 million from the PRC and Eastern Europe.[12]

Effects of sanctions on the economy

Evaluation of the effects of these regional sanctions on the Cuban economy is made more difficult because of the simultaneous social and economic revolution which affected all areas of activity.[13] The island has a population of approximately 8 million, of whom 57 per cent are urbanized, a high proportion by Latin American standards. Under United States influence after 1898, the cultivation of sugar and tobacco was undertaken on large estates. Before the revolution in 1959, about 20 to 25 per cent of Cuban land was owned by the sugar companies, half the arable land was used for sugar cultivation, and the industry employed 50,000 people. There is a good road and rail system and mineral deposits of chrome, nickel, and iron ore, but no domestic supply of oil, and hydroelectric potential is very small. Dependence on imported energy has been a major problem.

After Castro took power, the means of production were nationalized, and a central planning system installed. American assets were expropriated, and the state took over both agricultural and nonagricultural activities, including oil refining. Collective farms were established and an attempt made to diversify agriculture by growing new food crops and raising cattle.

Sugar was the chief export crop and mainstay of the Cuban economy, which was virtually monocultural. The United States formerly bought approximately 3 million tons per year, one half of the total crop. Out of total export earnings of $617.3 million in 1960, sugar contributed $467.5 million (over 75 per cent) while tobacco and tobacco manufactures, the next most important earners of foreign exchange, contributed only $63.0 million.[14]

The reduction of the United States sugar quota to zero in 1960 forced a drastic re-orientation of Cuba's external trade. Schreiber points out: "Because Cuba deliberately sought to end its trade dependence on the United States, some trade re-orientation would have occurred even if the US had not applied economic coercion, but the trade boycott made the break more complete than it would otherwise have been".[15] Unless sugar could be exported, imports, which accounted for 35 per cent of the gross national product in 1959, could not be financed. Import control was imposed in 1959 and consumer goods imports declined by 44 per cent in value between 1957 and 1962. But capital goods were essential not only for industrial development but for the re-equipment of the infrastructure supplied by the United States, for which parts were no longer available, and petroleum had to be imported to meet energy needs.

It was the loss of United States trade which was crucial; trade with the rest of Latin America declined, but except for the loss of imports of petroleum from Venezuela, this was not of such vital significance to Cuba.[16] After 1963 trade with Western Europe and Canada increased, and there was some growth in trade with Japan, Egypt, and Morocco but the leading role was played by the Soviet Union and other Communist countries which supplied the goods needed by Cuba and provided the credits required to finance their import. There has been a considerable expansion of the Soviet merchant fleet to handle Cuban trade; this was necessary because the US operated a blacklist of shipowners whose vessels carried cargoes to Cuba; no US government cargoes or government-financed cargoes could be carried in their ships.

In the three years from 1959 to 1962, the dominant position of the United States in Cuba's external trade·was eliminated. Whereas in 1959 the United States supplied 68 per cent of Cuban imports and took 69 per cent of Cuban exports, by 1962 Cuban trade with the United States was negligible; 82 per cent of Cuba's export trade and 85 per cent of her import trade was conducted with Communist countries, particularly the Soviet Union, Czechoslovakia, and mainland China. Under the terms of a bilateral trade agreement concluded in February 1960, the Soviet government agreed to buy 2.7 million tons of sugar and to increase purchases if the United States placed a total embargo on imports of sugar from Cuba. A long-term credit of $100 million was also extended. Relations between the Cuban and Soviet governments became very close and a long-term trade agreement concluded in 1963 provided for Soviet imports of sugar to increase by one million tons a year to a maximum of five million tons in 1968; imports would be maintained at that level until 1970. The price was fixed at 6c (US) per lb – lower than the ruling market price, but offering stability in earnings.

But in spite of this considerable support, supplemented by aid from other Communist countries in Europe and from mainland China, the Cuban economy experienced serious difficulties, particularly in the period 1961–64. For instance the US embargoes had an immediate effect on Cuba's port system, which was not equipped with facilities for handling ocean borne freight nor with adequate storage facilities.[17] An effort to break the traditional dependence on sugar led to an unwise diversification of productive activity and squandering of capital between 1961 and 1963. Sugar production declined sharply. From 1964 to 1970 Cuba came to depend even more heavily on Soviet economic aid and preferential trade arrangements,[18] and a swing to overemphasis on agriculture with an unrealistic target of 10 million tons of sugar production in 1970 followed the earlier overemphasis on industrialization. Commentators have concluded that the overall growth of the Cuban economy during the first ten years of revolution was almost nil, although redistribution of wealth brought greater social equality.[19]

The new import flows necessitated adaptation of production in all its stages: transport, distribution, and storage were all affected, as well as the upkeep or replacement of equipment originally or formerly bought from the United States, and throughout the 1960s Cuba ran an annual deficit with the Soviet Union which was never less than $100 million and at times nearly three times as high.[20] To reduce dependence on imported oil, the USSR assisted Cuba with the construction of a nuclear power station, and in recent years there have been marked improvements in the production of raw materials and manufactured goods and in mechanized harvesting methods, but any interruption of the supply of spare parts and semi-finished goods would be serious.

In January 1970 the author of an article in *Foreign Affairs* noted that there was no doubt "that the OAS policy of economic denial . . . has retarded, though it cannot entirely prevent, Cuba's economic development. More important still – and is this perhaps its main justification now? it has made more difficult the export of revolution . . . But . . . so long as the boycott continues, there will persist in this island a sort of siege mentality . . ."[21] In contrast, Blackburn writing in 1972 suggested that dependence "on Soviet economic assistance does not inhibit diversification and stimulation of the economy, as did dependence on the United States . . ."[22]

OAS sanctions were finally lifted in July 1975. The US maintains embargoes but there have been moves to normalize relations. In the mid-1970s, the participation of Cuban forces in the Angolan civil war and in Ethiopia's war with Somalia demonstrated a capacity to undertake foreign military adventures in spite of more than a decade of US/OAS embargoes, although Soviet military support was obviously necessary.

There have been no further cases of OAS sanctioning in the western hemisphere, although in the early 1970s Chile, under the Marxist government of Dr. Allende, became the object of heavy pressure from US multinationals such as ITT, Anaconda and Kennecott whose assets had been nationalized. Unlike Fidel Castro, who came to power through revolution and violence, Salvador Allende was elected by democratic process. Although his Marxist regime was highly unwelcome to the US, it would have been difficult to devise any legal justification for intervention through the mechanisms of the Rio Treaty, unless he undertook activities outside Chile which were perceived as threatening peace and security in the hemisphere. The difficulty of achieving OAS unanimity on Cuba (except during the missile crisis) and its reluctance to be associated with US intervention in the Dominican Republic in 1965, plus the further erosion of the leadership role of the US as a result of the Vietnam war, made any question of recourse to the OAS over Chile impractical. Nevertheless, the success of the internal and external forces opposed to Allende in bringing about his death in a right-wing coup in September 1973 are a melancholy reminder that overt or covert pressure which it would be hard to justify under international law may produce the results it seeks, while internationally authorized measures enjoying a greater degree of legitimacy may prove unavailing. There were widespread allegations of American complicity in the destabil-ization and overthrow of the Allende regime[23] and although hearings before the Senate Foreign Relations Committee's subcommittee on multinational corporations early in 1973 revealed that ITT's approaches to the CIA to prevent Allende's election had been rebuffed, and subsequent hearings found no evidence of US participation in the coup which led to his death, it is no secret that many forms of pressure were employed. In terms of the 1962 Hickenlooper Amendment to the Foreign Assistance Act, the US President is required to suspend aid to any government which expropriates American property without paying compensation and in 1972 the Gonzalez Amendment required US representatives in multilateral agencies to vote down loans in similar circumstances. Chile suffered accordingly as the World Bank and the Inter-American Development Bank refused new loans. Paul Sigmund notes the difficulty of distinguishing between "legitimate reasons for not making loans and credits available", which could be serious doubts about Chile's will and capacity to repay, and illegitimate ones which would relate to "defense of private corporations or in order to promote a military coup".[24]

The cases of economic coercion examined in this chapter have illustrated some of the difficulties of achieving success at the regional level. In the next two chapters attention will focus on the more comprehensive sanctioning efforts of the League and the United Nations.

4 Economic Sanctions under the League of Nations

In the system set up by the League of Nations in 1919 it was hoped that all states would be members and that they would respect each other's sovereignty and territorial integrity. Peace would be maintained under League auspices by arbitration, conciliation or resort to the new Permanent Court of International Justice, while disarmament would further reduce the likelihood of war. In addition, the Covenant provided for penalties, (or sanctions) for resort to war in breach of its provisions.

It was not originally envisaged that military and economic measures of enforcement would be used separately. Various drafts of the Covenant laid down a complete set of military and economic measures to restrain aggressors with whom members of the League would regard themselves as 'at war'. In other words, the full range of weapons which had been used in the recent war were to be available for use under League auspices to check further outbreaks of violence. In the first British Foreign Office (Phillimore) draft; "the economic weapon was considered simply as one of the incidental operations of war, . . ."[1] But General Smuts' pamphlet "The League of Nations: a Practical Suggestion" gave a prominent role to the economic boycott, and this fitted in well with President Wilson's idea, which had also been propounded by the American League to Enforce Peace and other groups sponsoring peace plans, that economic pressure could be substituted for military force as a means of maintaining peace. This optimistic view was summarized in the following words: "The economic weapon, conceived not as an instrument of war but as a means of peaceful pressure, is the great discovery and the most precious possession of the League."[2]

SANCTIONS AND THE LEAGUE SYSTEM

Enforcement under the Covenant was provided for in Article 16 which laid down an automatic sequence of events which would follow a specific form of illegal behaviour by a League member. Article 16(1) stated that if any member resorted to war, disregarding the obligations and procedures concerning pacific settlement of disputes laid down in Articles 12, 13, and 15, it was *"ipso facto . . .* deemed to have committed an act of war against all other Members of the League". They undertook "immediately to subject it to the severance of all trade or financial relations, the prohibition of all intercourse between their nationals and the nationals of the Covenant-breaking State, and the prevention of all financial, commercial or personal intercourse" between its nationals and nationals of third states.

The three succeeding clauses of Article 16 carried mutual cooperation and support in dealing with an aggressor to a further degree. Article 16(2) gave the League Council the "duty" of recommending "to the several governments concerned what effective military, naval or air force" members should contribute to "protect the Covenants of the League". In other words, the economic sanctions of Article 16(1) were to be backed up, if necessary, by force. Article 16(3) provided for mutual support in applying economic sanctions and cooperation in the use of force, and Article 16(4) contained provision for expulsion from the League by unanimous vote of the Council of any member who "violated any Covenant of the League".

It was recognised that the full application of Article 16 might have serious consequences for members; the potential backlash effect of economic sanctions on some states imposing them was seen to be considerable, particularly in view of the limited scope of League membership. A reluctance to be committed to far-reaching, unprofitable, and possibly damaging enforcement actions was shared by most states, and it was apparent even to contemporary observers that "most of the discussion of Article 16 among League members" was the result of apprehension regarding the scope of the commitment it imposed "rather than of a deliberate attempt to outline a programme for peace".[3]

As early as 1921, a series of interpretative resolutions was passed by the Assembly and accepted by the Council as guidelines for action in connection with Article 16. The result was a considerable dilution of the strength of that Article. For instance, it was no longer a question of automatic response to a breach of the Covenant; each member was henceforth to decide for itself whether a breach of the

Covenant had been committed. It was also recommended that economic pressure should precede resort to hostilities and should be graduated in application.

These resolutions, and subsequent studies of the implications of Article 16 – particularly in regard to relations with non-members of the League – revealed a general disinclination on the part of members to be committed in advance to the defence of any potential victim of aggression, or to the imposition of sanctions against any potential aggressor.

In the event, the practical experience of the League of Nations with economic sanctions was restricted to the single case of Italy. During the crisis caused by Japan's invasion of Manchuria in 1931, sanctions were neither applied nor officially discussed. The United States declined to recognize the new state of Manchukuo set up by Japan, and the League followed suit, but this negative political act was not backed by more positive measures, although the (Lytton) Commission of Enquiry sent by the League Council to study the situation in the Far East reported that Japan's military measures had been unjustified. Japan's reaction to the adoption of the Report was to give immediate notice of her withdrawal from the League.[4]

The Chaco war between Bolivia and Paraguay which began in 1928 also offered scope for possible League action.[5] Neither party to this long-drawn-out war could manufacture arms, and this lent weight to the argument for imposing a total embargo on exports of war material to both sides as a means of checking the fighting. A particularly violent phase of the struggle occurred in 1932 and an arms embargo was recommended by the League Council in 1934, but it was not fully implemented, and the smuggling of arms was rife. Parallel efforts to resolve the dispute were made by the Conference of American States and by neighbours of the belligerents, but in spite of all these efforts the war did not end until 1938.

The inaction of the League in the Far East, and its lack of success in Latin America, whatever justification might be advanced in each case, meant its virtual preoccupation with Europe. Following Hitler's announcement of German rearmament in 1935, the League Council set up a Committee of Thirteen to study measures to render the Covenant more effective in the organization of collective security. As this Committee proceeded with its work, it became clear that Italy, and not Germany, was the likely target of sanctions.

THE ITALO-ETHIOPIAN CASE

The importance of the Italo-Ethiopian crisis in the League's history is stressed by all authorities; whereas the implications of Article 16 had been exhaustively examined and analysed, there had been no attempt to activate it in previous crises. But on this occasion the League took action. Italy had invaded Ethiopia, in violation of her obligations under the Covenant and other international treaties, and was subjected to economic sanctions by the great majority of League members. The measures devised in 1919 were tested in practice, if only partially, for the first and only time.[6]

Course of the crisis

In examining the use of economic weapons in this instance it is not necessary to give a detailed account of the crisis, but consideration must be given to the political as well as the economic aspects of the sanctions experiment, if only because its collapse must be explained largely in terms of the indecisive action and ambivalent policies of the major League powers. Goals were too inconsistent, measures were too limited, the end of sanctions was sought too readily to make a convincing picture of a collective attempt to uphold the Covenant and protect Ethiopia from Italian aggression.

For Ethiopia the alternatives to going to the League for help would have been to seek an initial direct accommodation with Italy, or to attack Italian positions before Italy's preparations were complete. With hindsight, it is clear that her technically successful appeal under Article 15, which led to Italy's being subjected to sanctions in October 1935, was a hollow victory. Six months later, in May 1936, after a harsh campaign in which Ethiopian resistance was crushed, Italy announced the annexation of the whole country. Ethiopia could hardly have fared worse, and her fate was not lost on other small countries in the League system.

From December 1934, when the first border clash occurred at Wal-Wal between Italian and Ethiopian forces, until October 1935 when de Bono's forces began an intensive campaign in the field, events at Geneva were of less significance than the independent diplomatic manoeuvrings of France and Britain. The efforts of these two powers to obtain a settlement of the dispute were not centred on, or primarily channelled through, the League either in the opening or the closing stages of the crisis, nor indeed during the nine months from October 1935 to July 1936 when sanctions were officially in operation.

In the pre-sanctions period, the governments of these two countries were seeking understandings and assurances of support from Mussolini in the European context, and were anxious not to forfeit his goodwill by thwarting his colonial ambitions in Africa. Their overriding though ill-co-ordinated concern was the emergence of Germany, under Hitler, as a determined revisionist power, prepared to repudiate the Treaty of Versailles and threatening the peace of Europe. Mussolini was seen as a useful ally in the face of this threat. The affairs of Ethiopia took second place, and pressure was put on the Emperor from the outset to concede some of Mussolini's demands. Settlement of the dispute was also sought in terms of the tripartite Anglo-French-Italian treaty of 1906, outside League organs and procedures.

Ethiopia first appealed to the League Council under Article 11 in January 1935, but was persuaded to submit the Wal-Wal incident to arbitration under her 1928 treaty with Italy. Nothing having been accomplished, she invoked Article 15 of the Covenant on 17 March. On the same day, Hitler announced the re-introduction of conscription in Germany, in violation of the Treaty of Versailles. This seemed the greater peril and Britain, France and Italy, meeting at Stresa resolved to oppose unilateral treaty repudiation which endangered peace in Europe.

At an extraordinary meeting of the League Council in April this stand was endorsed and the Committee of Thirteen set up to study possible sanctions against treaty-breakers but no action was taken over Ethiopia. The next few months were occupied in attempts to establish an arbitration committee on the Wal-Wal incident; the growing tension between Italy and Ethiopia, and Italian military preparations in the Horn of Africa were ignored. The report of the arbitration committee absolved both sides from blame over Wal-Wal, and a more general examination of Italo-Ethiopian relations was put on the Council agenda for its meeting on 4 September. Italy's submission to this meeting of a document which described Ethiopia as a barbarous and uncivilized country, unfit to be a member of the League of Nations and unable to discharge her obligations under the Covenant, could not provide the legal or moral justification for her invasion of Ethiopia on a self-styled civilizing mission.

The last stage of this first phase of the crisis was marked by the completion of Italian military preparations, and by a distinct change of mood at the League in favour of decisive action. In Britain public opinion had rallied to the support of the League: the results of the Peace Ballot organized by the League of Nations Union showed that over ten million people supported the use of economic and other non-military measures to check aggression.[7] The British Foreign Secretary made what was taken to be a firm declaration of loyalty to the League at the meeting of the Assembly on 11 September, speaking of "steady and collective resistance to all acts of unprovoked aggression". Many other delegates spoke in the same vein, and it was clear that if Italy persisted in her plans and resorted to war against Ethiopia, sanctions would probably be invoked.

During September Italy rejected, and Ethiopia accepted, proposals made by the Council which could have formed a basis for settlement of their dispute. On 3 October 1935 Italy invaded Ethiopia. Immediately afterwards a Council Committee of Six reported that she had resorted to war in violation of her obligations under Article 12; the adoption of this report was the signal for the automatic application of sanctions under Article 16.

In the second, and decisive, stage of the crisis which followed the outbreak of hostilities, Italian forces subdued Ethiopia by using all the means of modern warfare, including gas, while the members of the League, led by Britain, belatedly and half-heartedly attempted to induce the Italian government to abandon its African adventure. For this objective to be achieved by economic measures it would have been necessary to bring Italy to a position where she was unable to carry on the campaign because of lack of resources, or found it unprofitable to do so because of economic hardship suffered at home.

It is true that important powers, notably the United States and Germany, were not members of the League, and that certain members did not co-operate in the sanctioning exercise. This lack of universality weakened the effect of sanctions. But the course of events revealed, first, a hesitancy on the part of Britain and France to sponsor the intensification of sanctions to a point where they might have been effective, and later, when the victory of Italian forces was complete, a significant readiness to abandon the sanctions policy and accept the *fait accompli*.

The sanctions which were imposed by League members comprised an embargo on the export of arms, munitions, and implements of war to Italy (Proposals I-IA); the restriction of financial dealings involving loans, credits, or share issues with government or business concerns in Italy (Proposals II-IIA); the prohibition of imports of Italian origin, with exemptions for books and printed material, gold, silver and coin, goods subject to existing contracts, and goods of Italian origin to which more than 25 per cent of value had been added by processing outside Italy (Proposals III-IIIA); a ban on the export to Italy of transport animals, rubber, bauxite, aluminium, iron ore, chromium, manganese, titanium, nickel, tungsten, vanadium, and tin (Proposal IV). Re-exports to Italy were also banned, but contracts in process of execution and goods already en route were exempt. A fifth Proposal related to the organization of mutual support.[8] "In nine days" writes Frank Hardie, "the committee had created, in outline, a new world of international sanctions",[9] but it should be noted that this was not the severance of communication and intercourse laid down in Article 16 of the Covenant, but a much more limited programme of denial which did not include the severance of diplomatic relations or any ban on travel.

It is possible that Italy's ability to succeed in Ethiopia could have been undermined had the Suez Canal been closed, cutting off Italian forces in East Africa from their home supplies. Britain was at that time the responsible power who would have had to enforce the closure. No government actually proposed this measure, although many outside groups did so; Mussolini is reported to have said he would regard it as an act of war. In fact, it had already been secretly agreed by the British and French governments that action against Italy would be limited to non-military measures.[10]

Much of the confidence which had been generated by the League in its relatively swift application of sanctions in the autumn of 1935 was lost after the disclosure of the terms of the Hoare-Laval Pact, drawn up privately in Paris in early December by the British Foreign Secretary and the French Prime Minister. This arrangement would have required Ethiopia to cede territory to Italy in the north, and to accept Italian economic expansion and settlement in the south. Although the plan had to be abandoned in the face of public reaction, and Hoare's resignation as Foreign Secretary followed, the damage to the sanctionist cause was considerable. The objectives of League action were confused, and the support of Britain and France for sanctions was called in question.

It was unlikely that severer sanctions would be imposed in the light of British government policy, expounded by the Under-Secretary for Foreign Affairs, to the House of Lords in the following words: "Therefore we do not in the least intend to take any action which Italy, for some reason obscure to us, although the Italians may think it quite clear, can interpret as isolated action done in hostility to Italy and which may cause us to find ourselves at war."[11]

Proposal IVA had acknowledged the expediency of additional embargoes "as soon as the conditions necessary to render this extension effective have been realized". The items included in Proposal IV had been limited to those controlled by the sanctioning group, due to uncertainty about the policy of the United States and other non-members of the League. Sanctions on oil, and other essential materials such as iron, steel, and coal were proposed by the Canadian delegate to the Committee of Eighteen in October, but at its January meeting these proposals were abandoned on the grounds that they would be ineffective. An expert committee, however, was set up to consider the effectiveness of an oil sanction. In its unanimous report issued on 12 February, this committee made the point that if an embargo on oil were to be universally applied, taking into account Italy's stocks, and supplies en route, the impact would be felt only after three and a half months. Moreover, effectiveness could be expected only if all members of the League participated and if the United States restricted its exports to the normal pre-sanctions level.[12]

In the meantime, Italy had made it clear that she would regard an oil embargo as an act of war and her forces were beginning to score military successes in Ethiopia. Once again, events in Europe intervened to divert attention from Africa: Hitler's re-occupation of the Rhineland on 7 March 1936, in breach of the Locarno Treaties and the Treaty of Versailles, led to a further meaningless statement from Britain, France and Italy expressing solidarity in the preservation of treaty obligations. It was clear that little weight could be attached to the British Foreign Secretary's statement to the Committee of Eighteen on 2 March to the effect that Britain would be prepared to join an oil embargo with other members who produced or shipped oil. Although the British government had been given electoral support for a firm stand on sanctions in the General Election held in November 1935, its concern for Italian friendship in Europe appears to have been overriding. France had been a reluctant partner in the sanctions front from the beginning.

Further efforts to achieve conciliation between Ethiopia and

Italy organized by the Council came to nothing. No extension of sanctions was proposed and the use of gas by Italian forces drew no more than a protest. Events moved swiftly in Ethiopia and on 2 May the Emperor was forced to flee the country. Mussolini declared the war was over and announced the annexation of Ethiopia on 9 May – two days before the next Council meeting. Consideration of the new state of affairs was postponed for a month while sanctions continued – then the matter was handed to the Assembly to deal with at a special session on 30 June.

The question was whether sanctions should be continued or abandoned and much depended on Britain's attitude. In a speech to Conservative MPs on 10 June, Chancellor of the Exchequer Neville Chamberlain declared that the continuation of sanctions would be the "very midsummer of madness"; the League's function, he said, should be limited and peace be secured by regional arrangements. A week later the Cabinet endorsed this position and it was upheld by Eden in the House of Commons.[13] At the Assembly, only South Africa and New Zealand were in favour of continuing sanctions; the question of recognizing the conquest of Ethiopia was dodged; the reform of the Covenant was canvassed. On 15 July the Sanctions Committee met to recommend the lifting of measures imposed under Article 16.

Economic effects of sanctions on Italy

Although the economic sanctions applied to Italy were neither well chosen nor effectively implemented, and their effect was considerably lessened by the political manoeuvres which accompanied them, the League attempt is worth examining in economic terms as an unprecedented programme of economic restraint imposed in time of peace by a group of fifty nations. It was predicted as early as 12 October 1935 that cutting off supplies to Italy would be "highly inconvenient" but not necessarily "crippling",[14] and this prediction proved to be well founded.

Italy appeared to be especially vulnerable to certain sanctions. Her population of 42 million lived in an area of less than 120,000 square miles, of which one-half was unfit for cultivation. Italy was not markedly deficient in food, and was an exporter of manufactures, but was seriously deficient in raw materials – particularly fuel in the form of coal and mineral oils. She needed to import cotton and wool for her textile industries, as well as timber, non-ferrous metals, iron and steel, and rubber. She was an important supplier of mercury and sulphur, but her main exports were of textiles and foodstuffs not indispensable to other countries.

Italy's adverse balance of trade was offset in the balance of payments by tourism, emigrants' remittances, and shipping receipts – items which were not eliminated by sanctions. She was capable of manufacturing armaments, given the necessary raw materials, and in this respect enjoyed a great advantage over Ethiopia.

During 1935 the build-up of strength for the war in Ethiopia had meant that the resources of the economy were stretched, and gold and foreign exchange reserves depleted. Exchange control was instituted and foreign securities in private hands were requisitioned. An import monopoly was established by the state for coal, copper, nickel, and other minerals. Later, private credits abroad were called in, dividends were limited, and taxes imposed on interest on bonds. These measures were primarily intended to save foreign exchange and find funds for government spending; when it became apparent that sanctions might be imposed, their effect in conserving exchange became of additional importance. Moreover, heavy stocks of strategic raw materials were built up in the pre-sanctions period.

Statistics of Italy's external trade in 1934 show that her six leading trade partners were Austria, France, Germany, Switzerland, Britain and the United States. The latter was the dominant supplier of wheat (58 per cent), of cotton and cotton goods (58 per cent), and an important source of iron and steel goods, mineral oils, and copper. Germany supplied 47 per cent of Italy's total coal imports, and over 50 per cent of machinery imports. Forty per cent of Italy's steel requirements came from non-sanctionists. The only raw material for which League powers were the dominant suppliers was wool. Italian exports were well distributed in different markets, a factor which reduced her vulnerability to sanctions.

When sanctions were imposed their economic impact was clearly much reduced by the non-co-operation of Austria and Hungary and the neutral policies of the United States, Germany, and Switzerland.

The United States administration placed an embargo on the export of arms and asked for moral embargoes on trading with the belligerents, but it was not empowered to place legal restraints on external commerce. The Hoare-Laval Pact is considered to have killed any prospects of the United States neutrality legislation being extended to give the administration powers to embargo exports of strategic materials. Germany embargoed the export of arms to Italy, but otherwise pursued a policy of 'normal' trade.

Figures published by the League show that the ban on exports of strategic raw materials (rubber, iron ore, aluminium, nickel and tin) was largely effective by December 1935. But heavy stocks of these commodities, and of oil, had already been built up by Italy, and the fact that military operations in Ethiopia were carried to a successful conclusion showed that these embargoes were not effective. The mineral sanctions might have been more effective if semi-manufactured goods had been included, and if there had been time for them to take effect. As it was, prohibited steel goods came from Germany, Austria, and the United States, while permitted goods came from France and the Soviet Union.

Italian exports fared badly under sanctions. Because of the exemption of contracts in process of execution, the embargoes on Italian goods did not take effect until early in 1936, but a drop in the value of total exports of 50 per cent was recorded in the next few months.

The embargoes on Italian exports were intended to aggravate Italy's shortage of foreign exchange, and as a result of the drop in exports, overseas purchasing power was reduced by two-fifths between December 1935 and February 1936, although Italy could still export gold and silver bullion and coin by depleting her reserves. Some re-orientation of foreign trade was achieved, but exports formerly sent to sanctionists were not wholly made up in non-sanctionist markets. Germany gained new markets at Italy's expense which were retained after sanctions ended.

Official statistics were not published in Italy after September 1935 but the re-organization of Italian industry by nationalization, and state control of the banking system, instituted in March 1939, indicated strains in the economy. All public issues of capital had to be approved by the Bank of Italy after that date; industry was to work for the armed forces of the state. At the end of March the Governor of the Bank of Italy announced that between 20 October and 31 December 1935 gold reserves had fallen from 3,936 million lire to 3,027 million lire, although reserves of foreign exchange remained stable at 370 million lire. The lira was devalued by 25 per cent in November 1935. League questionnaires showed gold imports from reporting countries in the first quarter of 1936 as totalling 1,092 million lire. This suggests that Italy lost half her gold reserve between October 1935 and March 1936, but gold was collected internally, and foreign assets could also have been realized.[15]

On 19 May 1936 the Italian Minister of Finance estimated that the import surplus averaged 213 million lire per month between December 1935 and March 1936. There is no reason to suppose he would have overestimated this figure. "By the end of the sanctions period it was reckoned that Italy's outstanding commercial debt had mounted to 1,500 million lire",[16] and Italy was finding difficulty in paying for goods even from non-sanctionist countries. Her balance of payments was showing considerable strain and stocks of raw materials were depleted. One-third of her total disposable international assets at the end of September 1935 was realized in the ensuing six months; there was a loss of shipping and tourist receipts, and the heavy cost of the war added to the strain.

The financial restraints imposed under Proposal II were not of great significance, as ordinary remittances were not affected, and Italy's lack of credit-worthiness had already made her a poor candidate for loans in the City of London.[17]

Economic effects on sanctionists

Effects on the trade of sanctionist countries took some time to show themselves, but for several months normal trading patterns were disrupted. The war and League action drove commodity prices up and stock markets lost ground temporarily in the third quarter of 1935, partly because of the strict implementation of the sanctions policy concerning imports from Italy, and partly because of an effective Italian counter-embargo on British goods.[18] The replacement of South Wales coal by German coal brought hardship to an area already suffering from high unemployment. French imports from Italy, like Britain's, fell heavily between November 1935 and January 1936, but her exports, though reduced, were not eliminated. Britain had to carry the additional cost of holding the fleet in readiness for war in the Mediterranean for eight months.

Yugoslavia was particularly hard hit as she was accustomed to send 21 per cent of her exports to Italy and 80 per cent of this trade was lost. Assistance under Proposal V was of little value.

The experiment in retrospect

The lessons to be learned from this ill-fated experiment were largely political. Lack of consensus on the merits of collective action to check aggression was apparent from the earliest days of the League; where Italy was concerned, consistent goals were neither clearly stated nor pursued – or perhaps perceived.

Any deterrent effect of sanctions was lost by a failure to warn Mussolini in clear terms that they would be applied if Italy did not refrain from aggression in Ethiopia; their practical effect was diminished by the failure to embargo vital raw materials or to sever communications. The Suez Canal was left open, tourism was not banned, an air service between Italian Somaliland and Eritrea continued to enjoy landing and refuelling rights in British Somaliland throughout the crisis. Undue reliance may have been placed on the embargo on imports from Italy, which Eden particularly advocated as the key measure which would leave Italy without foreign purchasing power and unable to obtain vital imports, and it is true that uncertainty about the co-operation of the United States and Germany made it difficult to know whether an embargo on strategic materials such as coal, oil, iron and steel would have been effective. It was obvious, however, that if these items were not subject to control by the sanctionists, Italy's war-making capacity would not be seriously reduced. Mussolini is reported by Hitler's interpreter to have said in 1938 that if the League had extended sanctions to include oil, he would have had to withdraw from Ethiopia "within a week".[19]

If a policy of economic pressure was being seriously followed, the selection of commodities for embargo of which the supply was largely controlled by sanctionist states, regardless of whether or not they were in short supply in Italy, could hardly be defended as rational. Similarly, an embargo on the supply of arms and munitions was meaningless for a country which manufactured and exported armaments.

The policy of graduated pressure, laid down in Proposal IVA, may have been acceptable on grounds of economy of effort, using only as much pressure as was needed, and avoiding undue disruption of trade, but it also gave Mussolini the opportunity to declare that extensions to sanctions would be regarded as hostile acts. His threats were probably not without effect; no extensions to the original sanctions were ever agreed upon.

"Collective bluffing cannot bring collective security"[20] – the comment of a Commonwealth Prime Minister at the end of the sanctions experiment – was an apt reflection on the League's experience under British and French leadership. Their "dual policy"[21] was doomed to failure. Inaction over Ethiopia might have damaged the League's reputation, but the sanctions venture hardly enhanced it, particularly as the target of collective action not only achieved its goals in triumph, but remained a member of the organization whose code it had flouted for as long as it chose to do so. In terms of the obligations of the Covenant, expulsion of Italy from the League would have been a more appropriate act than discussing whether the Ethiopian delegate had a right to take his seat after the conquest of his country.[22]

The failure of sanctions against Italy accelerated the rate of decline of the League. Attempts to reform it in the years from 1936 to 1939 were concerned more with limiting the obligations which it placed on members than with strengthening its powers.[23] Sterile debates about the respective merits of optional or compulsory sanctions served only to underline the fundamental lack of consensus about the League's true function. Events overtook debate at Geneva, which had become a political backwater.

The only sanctioning act taken after 1936 was the expulsion of the Soviet Union in 1939, following her attack on Finland. This gesture came after the outbreak of war in Europe. Eleven members left the League between 1936 and 1939 and four more during the war. The League Council did not meet again until 1945 when it formally dissolved the organization and named the United Nations as its successor. The experience of the United Nations with economic measures of coercion is considered in the next chapter.

5 United Nations Sanctions

When the UN Charter was drawn up in 1945, enforcement action, described as "effective collective measures for the prevention and removal of threats to the peace and for the suppression of acts of aggression or other breaches of the peace" was given a prominent place in Article 1(1). Members agreed to settle their disputes by peaceful means and to refrain from the threat or use of force in their relations with others. They further bound themselves to assist the UN in every way, to refrain from giving assistance to a state being subjected to preventive or enforcement action by the Security Council and specifically, in terms of Article 25, to carry out its decisions.

On paper, the Security Council was given executive capacity with power to investigate any situation which might lead to friction or give rise to a dispute endangering peace (Article 34) and to recommend appropriate procedures for, or terms of settlement. (Articles 36–7). Failing pacific settlement, Chapter VII of the Charter covering enforcement action is relevant. Here, unlike the League Council, the Security Council has very wide powers. It may determine the existence of any threat to or breach of the peace or act of aggression and make recommendations or decide what measures shall be taken to deal with the situation (Article 39). Given agreement among the permanent members and the necessary two-thirds majority vote, there would be no impediment to action. The exclusion from UN concern of matters falling essentially within the domestic jurisdiction of members does not apply in the case of enforcement action.

The highly developed economic warfare practised by the Allies from 1939 to 1945 again lent credence to the effectiveness of non-military measures of coercion, listed in Article 41 as the "complete or partial interruption of economic relations and of rail, sea, air, postal, telegraphic, radio and other means of communication, and the severance of diplomatic relations". Provided the use of armed force is not involved, the Security Council may also devise other measures under this article.

Agreements to make military contingents available to the Security Council for use if measures under Article 41 "would be ... or have proved to be inadequate" have never been concluded, so that military measures can be organized by the Security Council only on an ad hoc basis. Demonstrations of force and blockade both come into this category.

Early in the Charter, it is provided that the object of preventive or enforcement action may be suspended from exercising the rights and privileges of membership (Article 5) while the penalty of expulsion may follow persistent violation of the principles of the UN (Article 6). In addition, Article 94 gives the Security Council discretionary power to recommend or decide on measures to give effect to judgments of the International Court of Justice. The Charter also allows for enforcement action by regional agencies, but only with the authorization of the Security Council (Article 53). Collective self-defence is permitted under Article 51.

It is at the UN level that one might expect to find sanctions at their most convincing. As we have seen, regional organizations may reflect the norms of the dominant power and alternative value systems may be reinforced from outside the region. But the apparent strength of the UN enforcement system soon revealed flaws; stalemate in the Security Council follows the exercise of a veto by any permanent member and the attempt to shift emphasis to the General Assembly through the Uniting for Peace Resolution (1950) proved to be of limited usefulness. The Assembly can only recommend measures and cannot serve as a means of bringing effective pressure on either of the superpowers. Moreover, the supervisory role of the Security Council over regional bodies such as the OAS, the Arab League and the OAU, has not been exercised and these bodies have asserted a virtual autonomy in sanctioning not envisaged in the Charter. The UN reflects the divisions among its members and has obviously not functioned as a genuine collective security system. Consensus on generalized norms, such as 'peace' and 'non-discrimination', does not lead to common perceptions of failures to meet them; still less to agreement on measures to deal with offenders. As a result, Chapter VII has rarely been used and no systematic pattern of enforcement has developed.

NORTH KOREA AND CHINA

If the ineffective diplomatic measures against Spain recommended by the General Assembly in 1946 are ignored, the first application of collective measures under the Charter followed the North Korean attack on South Korea in June 1950. Due to the voluntary absenteeism of the Soviet Union, the Security Council was able to recommend military action, although it had no power to make it mandatory since agreements covering the use of force had not been concluded under Article 43. A breach of the peace was declared to have occurred; the immediate cessation of hostilities was called for; and members were called upon to render every assistance to the United Nations.[1] A further resolution asked specifically for members' assistance to the Republic of South Korea to repel armed attack and restore international peace and security in the area.[2] Military measures were organized under United States command and with the United States providing the bulk of the force. Fifty-three nations expressed willingness to support collective security in principle, but only sixteen offered military contingents.

The intervention of Communist China on the side of North Korea in October of the same year posed a new problem. By this time the Soviet Union had resumed attendance at Security Council meetings, and vetoed further action. The matter was transferred to the General Assembly which, acting under the Uniting for Peace Resolution, tried without success to effect conciliation and then passed a resolution naming China an aggressor. A Good Offices Committee was charged with the duty of seeking a peaceful solution, while an Additional Measures Committee was to report on further measures that could be taken. By May 1951 it was clear that peaceful settlement was not possible, and the Assembly recommended "additional" economic measures comprising an embargo on shipment to areas controlled by Communist China and North Korea of arms, ammunition and implements of war, atomic energy materials, petroleum, transportation materials of strategic value, and items useful for producing military materiel.[3] This general embargo was already broadly effective in so far as Western powers were concerned under existing strategic embargoes on trade with Communist countries; the Soviet bloc did not support the resolution. The first United Nations experiment with collective measures of an economic nature was therefore incomplete, indecisive, and inconclusive. The embargoes were ancillary to the military effort and could be of only limited effect since China could, at that time, obtain military equipment from the Soviet Union and other Communist countries. The Korean armistice in July 1953 brought an end to all United Nations measures, though not to the Western embargoes.

Subsequent crises in the Middle East, the Congo, Cyprus, and many other parts of the world have been referred to the United Nations, and peacekeeping efforts have been made on the initiative of its organs (and with the consent of the parties to disputes) with varying degrees of success. The Assembly voted that the Soviet Union was guilty of aggression in Hungary; the Soviet Union proposed collective action in the Suez crisis; there was discussion of the possibility of using economic sanctions against Katanga. Yet none of these crises brought compulsory enforcement under Chapter VII and the application of sanctions by the Security Council. In the course of the past two decades sanctions have been discussed both inside and outside the United Nations almost exclusively in relation to Southern Africa.

As former African colonies gained their independence and became full members of the United Nations they lost no opportunity of expressing their opposition to the continuation of "colonialism" in Southern Africa, where white minority governments ruled over African majority populations. Viewing the continuance of this state of affairs as a threat to the peace in terms of Article 39 of the Charter, they pressed for the application of economic sanctions against Portugal, the Republic of South Africa, and Rhodesia. They also organized regional boycotts under the auspices of the Organization of African Unity.

PORTUGAL

From 1961 a series of resolutions was passed by the General Assembly calling for economic sanctions against Portugal with the object of inducing the Portuguese government to accept the principle of self-determination for the inhabitants of its African territories. In 1965 the Assembly recommended that a wide range of sanctions should be imposed, including the breaking of diplomatic relations, the closing of ports to Portuguese vessels, and a boycott of trade; in 1966 that the Security Council should apply sanctions against Portugal under Chapter VII of the Charter. Western powers did not support this view, and the Security Council merely passed two recommendatory resolutions calling for a ban on the sale or shipment of arms and military equipment, and of materials for the manufacture of military materiel which could be used for the suppression of indigenous people in Portuguese Overseas African Territories.[4] There was no evidence that these recommendations were carried out by United Nations members, or that Portuguese policy was modified as a result of them. Portugal is a member of NATO, and strategic and trade links with the West may be presumed to have taken precedence over Assembly resolutions which Western countries did not even support.

The catalyst for change in the Portuguese African territories was the mounting strain of full-scale guerrilla warfare in both Angola and Mozambique and increasing discontent in Portugal which culminated in the coup which ousted the Salazar regime in April 1974. Independence for Angola and Mozambique in 1975, though not free from violence in the former case, brought an end to white rule and thus to censure at the UN. Indeed, it added two new members at the UN advocating change in Rhodesia and South Africa and considerably worsened the position of the Rhodesian government.

SOUTH AFRICA

The issues of apartheid[5] and the international status of Namibia (South West Africa) have been prominent on UN agenda for thirty years, and calls for economic sanctions have been unremitting. In the face of rapid progress in decolonization and the eradication of racial discrimination to which African states, and indeed most of the world, are pledged, apartheid in South Africa and its denial to non-white people of a share in effective government and equal rights before the law make it a provocative and dangerous element in international relations. The granting of 'independence' to the Transkei and two other much more fragmented 'homelands' together with some modifications in petty apartheid have not convinced governments of Afro-Asian countries of any change of heart among the ruling elite in South Africa and after South Africa's intervention in the Angolan civil war in 1975–76, an earlier trend in the 1970s which indicated some success for Prime Minister Vorster's policy of detente with African governments was reversed.[6]

The grounds for UN concern with apartheid are twofold: the possibility of a threat to the peace and the question of the denial of human rights. As the 'new' Commonwealth came to include an increasing number of Asian and African states, pressure mounted to exclude South Africa from international bodies. Faced with this hostility, South Africa withdrew from the Commonwealth on becoming a republic in 1961 and resigned or was excluded from a number of regional and functional agencies, including the UN Economic Commission for Africa, UNESCO, the Food and Agricultural Organization and the International Labour Organization.[7]

The General Assembly has passed many resolutions condemning South Africa's continued application of apartheid and failure to observe international obligations. After the disturbances at Sharpeville and other centres in South Africa in 1960, the matter was taken up by the Security Council which laid the blame for African loss of life on the South African government's racial policies; recognizing that the situation might endanger international peace and security it called upon the South African government to abandon apartheid.[8] Britain and France abstained from voting. Measures amounting to sanctions were first recommended by the General Assembly in 1962 when members were requested "separately or collectively, in conformity with the Charter" (a) to break diplomatic relations with South Africa or refrain from establishing them; (b) to close ports to ships flying the South African flag; (c) to forbid their ships to enter South African ports; (d) to boycott South African trade; (e) to refuse landing or passage facilities to aircraft belonging to the government of South Africa or companies registered in that country.[9] By the same resolution, the Assembly established the Special Committee on Apartheid to keep the racial policies of the South African government under continuous review and requested the Security Council to take appropriate measures, including sanctions and not excluding expulsion, to secure South Africa's compliance with UN resolutions.

The Security Council followed up the Assembly's action in 1963 with a resolution which described the situation in South Africa as "seriously disturbing" international peace and security (deliberately avoiding the terminology of Article 39) and solemnly calling on all states to cease forthwith the sale and shipment to South Africa of arms, ammunition of all types and military vehicles.[10] Voting was 9:0. Britain and France again abstained. A proposal for a trade boycott was defeated. Meanwhile, reports of the Special Committee on Apartheid were being submitted and studied and there was evidence of more unrest in South Africa. In December 1963 the Security Council reiterated its call for a ban on arms sales to South Africa, adding equipment and materials for the manufacture of arms to the list. It also authorized the Secretary-General to appoint a group of experts to examine methods of resolving the South African problem.[11] This resolution was notable in that, for the first time, Britain and France voted in favour, instead of abstaining; it was therefore adopted unanimously. However, the governments of both countries qualified their position on the arms embargo by stating that they would distinguish between items to be used for internal suppression and items to be used for external defence; the latter would continue to be supplied. The Labour government which took office in Britain in October 1964, banned all arms exports to South Africa immediately.

In April 1964, the report of the Group of Experts recommended a National Convention "fully representative of the whole population of South Africa" to set a new course for the future – a proposal which was promptly rejected by the South African government. The Group also recommended an expert examination of the economic and strategic aspects of sanctions. Acting on this suggestion, the Security Council reaffirmed its call for all members to observe the ban on the sale of military equipment, and set up an Expert Committee to study the feasibility of sanctions against South Africa. Its report was issued the following year.[12] It was clear from the comments of participants in the deliberations of the Expert Committee, and from memoranda submitted to it, that South Africa's major trading partners were opposed to any programme of economic restraints, and the final vote of six to four against sanctions was a blow to the international boycott movement.

The OAU, established in 1963, had also recommended sanctions against South Africa to its members; diplomatic links were severed – or not established, trade was officially boycotted, and overflying rights denied to South African planes.

South Africa's unwillingness to place the mandated territory of South-West Africa (renamed Namibia by the UN in 1968) under international trusteeship or to grant it independence, and her failure to apply mandatory sanctions to Rhodesia provided further grounds for international censure. In 1966 following the World Court's decision that Ethiopia and Liberia had not demonstrated sufficient material legal interest to bring their case challenging South Africa's administration of Namibia before the Court, the General Assembly voted 114:2 with 3 abstentions, to terminate the mandate for Namibia and place the territory under UN administration.[13] The Assembly's action was upheld in subsequent Security Council resolutions[14] and by an Advisory Opinion given by the ICJ at the Security Council's request in June 1971 which declared South Africa's continued presence in the territory to be illegal.[15]

UDI in Rhodesia in 1965 presented South Africa with a new problem in its relations with African states and with the UN. Initially, though perhaps regretting the Smith government's act in severing links with Britain which precipitated international intervention, South Africa gave full support to Rhodesia, continuing normal trade and friendly relations and only withholding formal recognition of independence. No doubt the South African government was anxious that economic sanctions should fail and be seen to fail, as this would discourage their use against the Republic; moreover there was strong popular support for Rhodesia among South African whites. The South African opposition wanted the government to extend recognition to the Rhodesian regime.

But as time passed, and opportunities for settlement with Britain were lost, first by the Rhodesian government's intransigence and later in 1972 by the Rhodesian African people's rejection of the settlement proposals worked out by the two governments, Rhodesia became a burden to South Africa. In the early 1970s the South African government was exploring the possibilities of "detente" with African states and was therefore not so anxious to be bracketed with Rhodesia; in 1974 the coup in Portugal followed by independence for Angola and Mozambique brought a new balance of power in Southern Africa and South Africa openly put pressure on the Rhodesian government to achieve a settlement with Britain. It withdrew its para-military forces from Rhodesia in 1975 and participated in various international conferences and meetings in respect both of Rhodesia and Namibia to which it decided to grant independence in 1978 hoping for a "compatible" government.[16] But pressure at the UN did not let up. In 1974 in the Assembly a vote of 91:22 confirmed the President's rejection of the credentials of the South African delegation; in the same year, Britain, France and the United States vetoed a Security Council resolution to expel South Africa from the organization, and they have continued to block the imposition of mandatory sanctions.

Western members of the Security Council, (the US, West Germany, Britain, France) have co-operated with South Africa in trying to devise a formula for elections in Namibia in which the South-West African People's Organization (SWAPO) – recognized by the UN as representing the Namibian people – would participate, while Anglo-American initiatives, with South African support, sought to bring about a peaceful transfer of power to the African majority in Rhodesia. But the 1978 internal constitutional settlement and subsequent elections which led to black majority rule in the Rhodesian parliament and a new government headed by Bishop Muzorewa have not been accepted by Britain and the US as a basis for recognition, or by the Patriotic Front as justification for ending the guerrilla war. The peaceful resolution of Zimbabwe-Rhodesia's future is still in doubt at the time of writing, and earlier hopes that Namibia would move to independence in 1979, with a UN Transitional Assistance Group of 7,500 stationed in the territory to supervise elections and monitor South African and SWAPO forces, have also faded.

In spite of South Africa's moves to "disengage" itself from Namibia and Rhodesia, international pressure on the Republic has not relaxed and when her two northern neighbours are under black rule, one can expect an intensification of effort at the United Nations to bring an end to apartheid. In 1976 riots in Soweto and other parts of South Africa and continued evidence of harsh treatment of blacks who demanded equal rights in their own country led to a Security Council resolution which declared the arms trade with South Africa a 'threat to the peace' under Article 39 of the Charter.[17] Arms sales to South Africa from any member of the UN are now illegal in terms of this resolution and France, which had previously ignored Security Council recommendations in this respect announced in August 1977 that although existing contracts would be fulfilled, no further sales would be permitted.

The resolution was so phrased that it became self-liquidating; it was the arms trade, not apartheid which was deemed a threat to the peace; presumably compliance by UN members ends the threat. Apartheid has been called many things and has been denounced many times, but it has not yet attracted an Article 39 determination by the Security Council which would mean mandatory political and economic sanctions. Western powers have vetoed such resolutions in the past and will presumably continue to do so as long as they are not ready to sacrifice economic links with the Republic in the cause of human rights. But members of OAPEC did impose a total oil embargo on supplies to South Africa in November 1973 (see Chapter 3 above) and it is above all in this respect that South Africa is vulnerable. The Republic has many economic strengths: it does not import food; it is the world's largest producer of gold besides producing a wide range of important minerals; it has a powerful and highly developed industrial sector; and abundant technical and managerial skills. It is becoming increasingly in-dependent of imported capital and is approaching the point where it can manufacture most of her domestic requirements except those with a very high technological content. South Africa's defence forces are strong and well equipped, and its capacity to impose counter-sanctions is considerable. The country is, however, par-ticularly vulnerable to an oil embargo, having no domestic source of supply (except for a limited oil from coal enterprise) and being heavily dependent on imported oil for essential civilian and military needs, particularly in transportation. South Africa's vulnerability to external economic pressure and measures the government has taken to reduce it are discussed further in Chapters 6 and 7 below.

RHODESIA

The Rhodesian case is unique in the record of the United Nations in that a wide range of mandatory economic sanctions was imposed by the Security Council under Chapter VII of the Charter to deal with a situation defined as constituting a threat to the peace.[18]

The unilateral declaration of independence by the Rhodesian government on 11 November 1965 followed months of protracted negotiation with Britain on the question of the territory's consti-tutional future, while at meetings of the United Nations, Common-wealth Prime Ministers and the Organization of African Unity there was continued pressure on Britain not only to forestall or prevent UDI, but to assume a more direct responsibility for African political advancement in Rhodesia.

It is not necessary in this context to recount in detail the background to the Rhodesian crisis, nor to relate the history of the short-lived Federation of Rhodesia and Nyasaland which was finally dissolved at the end of 1963.[19] It is relevant, however, to summarize briefly the issues at stake, which led to the imposition of 'voluntary' sanctions by Britain and many other countries immediately after UDI, and, one year later, to the decision of the Security Council to impose mandatory economic sanctions.

The break-up of the Federation was followed in 1964 by the independence and admittance to the Commonwealth and United Nations of Zambia (formerly Northern Rhodesia) and Malawi (formerly Nyasaland), both ruled by African governments. Rhodesia (formerly Southern Rhodesia),[20] which had enjoyed full internal self-government since 1923 with white minority rule, came out of Federation well in material terms, but independence was to be granted only when African participation in government was further advanced. In the meantime the 1961 Constitution, which gave limited and qualified franchise to Africans, was to continue in force. Independence was the declared aim of the Rhodesian Front Party which had defeated the United Federal Party in December 1962, and was to eliminate it as a Parliamentary Opposition in May 1965. A referendum on independence in November 1964 produced an 89 per cent vote in favour, although only 60 per cent of the electorate voted; this followed a warning from the newly elected Labour government in Britain that an illegal declaration of independence by Southern Rhodesia would cut her off from Britain, the Commonwealth, most foreign governments and international organizations, and bring disastrous economic damage.

Negotiations with the British government on the independence issue centred around five principles which Britain insisted must be accepted. A sixth principle was added by Mr. Wilson in January 1966, after UDI. These six principles were as follows:

1. The principle and intention of unimpeded progress to majority rule, already enshrined in the 1961 Constitution, would have to be maintained and guaranteed.

2. There would also have to be guarantees against retrogressive amendment of the Constitution.

3. There would have to be immediate improvement in the political status of the African population.

4. There would have to be progress towards ending racial discrimination.

5. The British Government would need to be satisfied that any basis proposed for independence was acceptable to the people of Rhodesia as a whole.

6. It would be necessary to ensure that, regardless of race, there was no oppression of majority by minority or of minority by majority.[21]

Stalemate was reached in the autumn of 1965, in spite of a

personal visit to Salisbury by Mr. Wilson in late October. The atmosphere of crisis mounted in early November when the Rhodesian government declared a three-month State of Emergency and imposed general import controls. A last appeal by Mr. Wilson was ignored and on 11 November, UDI was announced, thus confronting the British government with a *fait accompli*.

Reaction to UDI

Official reaction in Britain was sharp. On the same day Mr. Wilson condemned the act as illegal and ineffective in law. He termed it an act of rebellion against Crown and Constitution and instructed the Governor of Rhodesia to inform the Rhodesian Prime Minister and his colleagues that they no longer held office. On paper, the British government took over full responsibility for the government of Rhodesia; legislative and executive authority was vested in the Crown (i.e. the Imperial government) in terms of the Southern Rhodesia Act passed on 16 November. But the use of force was not contemplated and it was not even held in reserve. Mr. Wilson had already stated categorically in the British House of Commons that under no circumstances would Britain assert military power, whether to suspend or amend the 1961 Constitution, to impose majority rule "tomorrow or any other time" or to deal "with the situation that would follow an illegal assertion of independence".[22]

Britain took the lead in imposing economic restraints which were announced progressively in the three months following UDI. A complete ban on imports into British territories of Rhodesian tobacco was imposed on 11 November, together with a ban on further purchases of Rhodesian sugar. Exports of petroleum and petroleum products were banned on 17 December 1965, a total ban on exports to Rhodesia, excepting only items of a humanitarian nature, books, films, requirements for Central African organizations, and goods on quays already paid for, was in force by 30 January 1966, and a total ban on imports by the end of February. Penalties were prescribed for illegal trading.

Financial measures included the removal of Rhodesia from the sterling area; her exclusion from membership of the Commonwealth preference area and the Commonwealth Sugar Agreement; the end of British financial aid; the prohibition of the export of capital to Rhodesia; and the closing of the London capital market for Rhodesian dealings. Current payments by residents of the

United Kingdom to Rhodesia were virtually stopped; Rhodesian sterling was blocked and could no longer be exchanged for foreign currency in Britain. Assets of the Rhodesian Reserve Bank, amounting to approximately £10 million were frozen in London; the governor and director were suspended and a new board appointed in Britain.

Commonwealth and other countries followed Britain's lead in severing or reducing economic links with Rhodesia. The Council of Ministers of the OAU announced a total economic boycott in December 1965, which included a ban on communication and denial of overflying rights. The United States and France imposed oil embargoes in December 1965 and the former also banned exports to Rhodesia in March 1966; France imposed restrictions on the import of tobacco and sugar.

In spite of these harsh economic measures, and the denial of recognition to the government of Rhodesia, it remained in full administrative control. Its practical competence was acknowledged by all Rhodesians from the outset and, subsequently, by the British government itself which on numerous occasions conducted negotiations for a settlement with Mr. Smith and his colleagues. The credibility of the British government's dismissal of the Rhodesian government was never established.

After UDI, pressure mounted on Britain to take the matter to the United Nations. At a special Commonwealth Conference in Lagos in January 1966, Mr. Wilson confidently predicted that measures taken by the British government would be adequate to restore legality in Rhodesia "within a matter of weeks rather than months"[23] – an over-optimistic assumption which was not to be fulfilled. At a second Commonwealth Conference in London in the following September, Britain was pressed by African members to adopt stronger action, and agreed that if the Rhodesian government did not take steps to end the rebellion by the end of the year – which would mean that 'voluntary' sanctions had not worked – Britain would withdraw previous offers for a constitutional settlement, would not consider any settlements which involved the granting of independence before majority rule and would take the matter to the Security Council.

Efforts to find a solution culminating in the Wilson-Smith meeting on HMS *Tiger* proved fruitless; the Smith regime was unwilling to make concessions and Britain reluctantly took the matter to the UN.

United Nations mandatory sanctions

The imposition of sanctions by the Security Council on 16 December 1966, brought a new phase in the crisis. Although the measures selected were not as extensive as those already in force on a voluntary basis in Britain and other Commonwealth and non-Commonwealth countries, they were mandatory for all United Nations members. Sanctions against Rhodesia would therefore provide the first real test of United Nations 'enforcement' using economic weapons.

The subject of Rhodesia had featured on United Nations agenda since 1962. Immediately prior to UDI, the Assembly had called upon Britain to employ all necessary measures, including military force, to deal with rebellion by the Smith government;[24] after UDI the Security Council called upon all states to cease providing the illegal regime with arms, equipment and military materiel, "and to do their utmost in order to break all economic relations with Southern Rhodesia". An embargo on the export of petroleum and petroleum products was particularly recommended.[25]

In April 1966, at the request of the British government, the Security Council took further action. In order to prevent oil reaching Rhodesia via the port of Beira from which a pipeline ran to Umtali, the Security Council invoked Article 39 of the Charter, authorizing Britain to intercept ships bound for Beira which were reasonably believed to be carrying oil destined for Rhodesia and prevent them from discharging their cargo, by force if necessary.[26]

The grounds for collective action against the rebel regime in Rhodesia were provided by Britain's decision, supported by resolutions of the Security Council and the General Assembly, that the rebellion was not only an illegal act, which should be put down by the constitutional authority (Britain), but one which had international implications and was legitimately the concern of the United Nations. That Britain acknowledged this fact from the beginning was clear from warnings that she would take the matter to the United Nations if the Rhodesian government did not come to terms; her subsequent recourse to the Security Council for authority to establish a blockade of Beira confirms it. The decision in December 1966 to impose mandatory sanctions under Articles 39 and 41 was taken with Britain's concurring vote, while France and the Soviet Union abstained. Politically, no permanent member had an interest in using the veto.

The sanctions imposed by Resolution 232 of 16 December 1966 banned the export of petroleum, arms, ammunition and military equipment, vehicles and aircraft; and imports from Rhodesia of tobacco, sugar, meat and meat products, asbestos, copper, chrome ore, iron ore, hides and skins – key commodities which made up 59 per cent by value of her export trade. Non-recognition of Rhodesia's self-styled independence continued to be universal.

The twin objectives of this policy were presumably to bring about a return to constitutional government and to ensure a rapid progression towards majority rule. External pressure was intended to induce radical internal change, a goal of a very different character from that of checking external aggression which was relevant in the case of League sanctions against Italy in 1935. In the Rhodesian case, economic pressure was expected to produce divisions in the electorate, leading to the capitulation of the Smith Regime, or to its fall and replacement by a more amenable group of leaders. Problems associated with the objectives of sanctioning powers in the Rhodesian and other cases are discussed further in the next Chapter.

Intensification of sanctions

In March 1968 the execution in Salisbury of three Africans, in defiance of a reprieve granted to them by the Queen, revealed Britain's impotence to control events in Rhodesia. There was a renewed demand at the United Nations for stronger measures to be taken against the Smith regime. After weeks of discussion, a resolution put forward by the British representative on the Security Council was adopted unanimously. It required UN members to prohibit:

1. The import of all commodities and products originating in Rhodesia.
2. Any activities by their nationals or within their territories which would promote the export of Rhodesia products.
3. Shipment of Rhodesian products or of goods destined for Rhodesia in ships or aircraft of their registration or under charter to their nationals, or carriage of such exports (whether or not in bond) across their territories by land transport.
4. The sale or supply by their nationals from their territories of any commodities or products to persons or bodies in Rhodesia, excepting only medical supplies, educational equipment and materials,

publications, new materials, and in special humanitarian circumstances, foodstuffs.

5. The provision of funds for investment or of any other financial or economic resources to government, commercial or industrial enterprises in Rhodesia, and the remittance of any funds to Rhodesia except for pensions or payment for items exempted from the export ban under 4 above.

6. The entry into their territories, except on exceptional humanitarian grounds, of any person travelling on a Rhodesian passport, regardless of the date of issue.

7. Airline companies constituted in their territories, or of their registration or under charter to their nationals from operating to or from Rhodesia, or from linking up with any airline company constituted, or aircraft registered, in Rhodesia.[27]

Further provisions of this resolution advocated the withdrawal of all consular and trade representation in Rhodesia and the discouragement of emigration to Rhodesia. Contracts or licences approved before the date of the resolution were to be invalidated if they contravened its provisions. States which had not complied with the earlier sanctions resolution of December 1966 were censured, and all members of the United Nations urged to render moral and material assistance to the people of Rhodesia in their struggle for freedom. This exhortation referred to the non-white population, and not to the whites who declared UDI.

A Committee of the Security Council was set up to examine the Secretary-General's reports on implementation of sanctions, and to seek further information from members or from specialized agencies regarding trade or activities which appeared to constitute an evasion of the measures decided upon.[28]

If Resolution 253 had been fully implemented it would have effectively closed the loopholes which, under Resolution 232 had, allowed Rhodesia to export certain commodities freely, and to import all items except petroleum, vehicles and aircraft, and military materiel. The crucial question was whether United Nations members and non-members would take decisive action to implement its terms, and particularly whether South Africa and Portugal would continue to hold Rhodesia's economic head above water.

Further negotiations between the British and Rhodesian governments, including another round of shipboard talks (on HMS *Fearless* in October 1968) proved equally unproductive; a major sticking point was the Rhodesian refusal to accept an external check on retrogressive amendment of the constitution which is ironic in the light of much greater concessions made in the late 1970s. In Rhodesia between 1965 and 1970 the move was to the right among whites and a new republican constitution published in 1969 and introduced after a referendum in 1970 worsened the position of Africans. This provoked a further crisis at the UN. African members called for the use of force, a ban on postal and telecommunications links with Rhodesia, and the extension of sanctions to Portugal and South Africa, but their efforts were frustrated by Britain and the US in the Security Council. The latter used its veto power for the first time on these issues. A compromise resolution stiffened sanctions again by calling for the severance of diplomatic and consular relations and of transportation links with Rhodesia.[29]

Another round of negotiations between Britain and Rhodesia produced proposals which the Pearce Commission put to the African people of Rhodesia in 1972, and which they rejected. Rhodesia continued to resist international censure and defy sanctions with some success. But the sands were running out for Portuguese rule in Angola and Mozambique and the coup in Portugal in 1974 was to usher in an era in which not only Rhodesia, but also South Africa, would be exposed to new and powerful pressures. Guerrilla warfare began in 1972, placing heavy additional strains on the Rhodesian economy and the confidence of whites began to crack, while the withdrawal of South African police forces from Rhodesia in 1975 signalled an obvious preference on the part of that country for a settlement to be reached in Rhodesia which would satisfy Britain and the US – even if that meant African majority rule.[30] By 1976 Ian Smith was ready to accept a transitional multi-racial government and majority rule in two years' time in return for the lifting of sanctions and the end of guerrilla warfare; the tragedy was that by the time Anglo-American initiatives were successful at the intergovernmental level, they were inadequate to satisfy all Rhodesian African leaders. Guerrilla warfare could not be turned off like a tap. The forces of Joshua Nkomo and Robert Mugabe, loosely associated in the Patriotic Front, had goals of their own which could only be met by military means and the war was escalating. Its cost in terms of human life was 12,000 dead by the end of 1978, nearly one half in the last twelve months of that period; agricultural regions were under attack and a number of serious incidents of terrorism, including the shooting down of Air Rhodesia planes and a fire in the Salisbury oil depot estimated to have cost about £10 million in foreign exchange had brought the war to the heart of white Rhodesia.

The effects of sanctions

In evaluating the role of UN sanctions against Rhodesia, the first and obvious conclusion must be that for as long as they were the main instrument of pressure they did not achieve the goal of ending UDI. This raises two questions: why they did not work, particularly during the early years, and what, if anything, they served to accomplish.

At UDI, the Rhodesian economy had certain built-in strengths: a subsistence agriculture sector (which supported about half the African population) and attainable self-sufficiency in food; considerable mineral resources including chrome ore and gold; an industrial base sufficiently developed to be rapidly expanded utilizing unused capacity; hydro-electric power in abundance. Its weaknesses were its landlocked position and dependence on foreign transport routes, dependence on foreign trade for 38 per cent of national income; concentration of export earnings on a few commodities, notably tobacco, and two markets (Britain and South Africa); the need to import petroleum which in 1965 represented 28 per cent of total energy requirements; and the numerical insignificance of the white population who wielded economic and political power but were outnumbered at least eight to one by Africans (a ratio which was worsening).[31] While all sections of the population suffered some hardship following sanctions, the government was particularly concerned to protect whites who were the source of electoral support. Government compensation schemes and other forms of financial assistance helped to maintain farmers' incomes. The African population took the brunt of sanctions and the growing level of African unemployment has been of serious consequence to the economy over the long period. A stagnant, or shrinking economy cannot cope with a situation where some thirty to forty thousand new entrants to the labour market need to find jobs each year. The increasing rate of white emigration, in spite of stringent controls on removal of assets, has also weakened the economy in recent years.

Detailed and reliable information about foreign trade has not been available from Rhodesia since UDI; up to 1972 the government published total export and import figures with no breakdown of composition or direction; thereafter no information whatsoever about foreign trade was disclosed. South Africa ceased to publish details of its 'African' trade after 1966. Statistics compiled by the UN Secretariat[32] show that Rhodesian exports fell from $399 million in 1965 to $238 million in 1967, but thereafter increased in value. In 1975 they were estimated at $645 million and in 1976 at $748 million. In 1976 information from reporting countries accounted for $65 million (the US accounting for $46 million and Switzerland $8 million); in addition the Secretariat calculated that South Africa and its Customs Union partners (Botswana, Lesotho, Namibia and Swaziland) took $365 million. This left $312 million unaccounted for, and these exports from Rhodesia were presumably sent to other countries through the South African Customs Union.

Rhodesia's export trade was concentrated in the relatively small range of primary commodities which were listed in Security Council Resolution No. 232 (1966), but it is clear that the sanctions were never fully effective and as time passed they became less so. Tobacco pre-UDI accounted for 30 per cent by value of Rhodesia's export trade ($132 million out of a total of $399 million in 1965) and as half the crop traditionally went to British markets, it was seen as a prime target for sanctions. Initially it was very badly hit and the Rhodesian government took urgent measures to assist farmers to stockpile while encouraging diversification into other crops. Sugar, like tobacco was placed under sanction by Britain in 1965, and here too, exports suffered at first, but agricultural exports, especially beef and beef products continued to find markets and the diversification of production, particularly into maize and wheat also strengthened Rhodesia's export trade. Even tobacco, which is identifiable as 'Rhodesian' proved exportable.[33] Minerals, particularly asbestos, nickel and chrome can and have been exported via South Africa; from 1971 to 1977 the US openly violated UN sanctions by importing chrome ore from Rhodesia under the Byrd amendment, the alternative being to import it from the USSR. Overall, the UN Secretariat concludes that in spite of sanctions Rhodesia "has been able to send its exports indirectly to world markets".[34]

Rhodesia's import trade was more widely diversified than her export trade; key commodities listed in the original sanctions resolutions were motor vehicles and parts, petroleum and petroleum products, and aircraft and parts. These were obviously strategic items, but they accounted for only 16 per cent of total

Rhodesian imports in 1965. The Secretariat has found it impossible to monitor Rhodesia's import trade, although it is well known that evasion of sanctions has been highly successful and this is discussed in more detail later in this chapter and in Chapter 7.

Secretariat estimates of the total value of Rhodesian imports in 1975 and 1976 were $588 million and $620 million respectively compared with $334 million in 1965 and $236 million in 1966. Recorded trade from reporting countries in 1976 accounted for $ 10 million (approximately 6 per cent of the total) while it is estimated that the South African Customs Union exported $246 million to Rhodesia. This suggests that over 50 per cent of Rhodesia's imports were obtained from outside the South African Customs Union despite sanctions.

It was obviously in the interests of the regime to keep the import bill as low as possible, and to use foreign currency for essential purposes. Sanctions gave a strong impetus to import substitution and the further development of manufacturing industry. Pre-UDI industrial activity was concentrated mainly in processing and packing of agricultural products, in textiles and clothing and the manufacture of building materials; there was also some output of furniture, paints and electrical appliances. After UDI manu-facturers concentrated on the home market, and in addition to expanding the lines noted above, production of crop-spraying and irrigation equipment, ceramics, breakfast cereals, confectionery and other products was successfully initiated. Locally grown cotton provided a base for the rapid expansion of the textile industry. Cotton handling and ginning facilities were developed, spinning and weaving expanded and the Rhodesian clothing industry prospered. At South Africa's instigation, controls were placed on the export of low-price clothing from Rhodesia to South Africa in 1968 – an indication of concern at the growth in competitiveness of the Rhodesian clothing industry.

In 1975 the index of volume of manufacturing production was 88 per cent above the 1965 level. But the small home market and the limits set on exports by sanctions have made it impossible for Rhodesian industry to expand profitably; in fact, a decline in the volume of exports was recorded in 1977 and 1978. Moreover, Rhodesia finds it necessary to import some capital goods and here sanctions present difficulties and add to costs. The balance of payments moved into deficit in 1977 and 1978 was expected to be another year of negative growth.

From the beginning, foreign exchange was a serious problem for the Smith regime and stringent controls were imposed. Rhodesian currency is convertible only in South Africa and this forced a variety of schemes for obtaining much needed foreign currency or for doing without it.[35] Exporting at a discount and importing at a premium added to the problem. In the early years after UDI, the blocking of financial transactions by Britain and later by the United Nations worked to Rhodesia's advantage in that it was able to repudiate external debts and retain dividends and profits within the country, but the need for foreign capital for development purposes has grown and cannot necessarily be met from South African sources. In 1965 tourism was the largest foreign exchange earner after tobacco, asbestos and copper and for some years the tourist industry held up well in spite of sanctions. But the insecurity produced by guerrilla warfare and terrorism dealt a blow to Rhodesia's tourist trade in the late 1970s. Reports of the UN Sanctions Committee have drawn attention to the sharp fall-off in foreign tourists since 1975; the number of visitors in January–June 1977 was one-third that for the comparable period in 1975.[36]

Part of the failure of sanctions can be attributed to defensive and adaptive measures taken by the Rhodesian government and supported by the white population, and by the capacity of the economy to respond to new needs. But it must also be emphasised that sanctions evasion considerably lessened their economic impact and the role of Portugal (until 1974) and South Africa has been crucial. The vital commodity was probably petroleum, and here the UN oil embargo was circumvented from the outset. Supplies were made available from South Africa on an emergency basis, and neither the closing of the Beira-Umtali pipeline (and the Ferukka refinery in Rhodesia) nor the limited blockade of Beira from April 1966 which was followed by the Security Council's decision to include petroleum among banned exports in December 1966, succeeded in depriving the Rhodesian economy of adequate supplies of refined petroleum. The UN Secretariat reported to the Security Council Sanctions Committee in 1976 that it was ". . . reasonable to assume that a steady flow, in sufficient quantity, of petroleum products to Southern Rhodesia through South Africa has continued to be efficiently arranged";[37] reports commissioned by the Commonwealth Committee on Southern Africa in 1977[38] and the British government in 1978[39] have made it quite clear how this was done through 'swap' or product exchange arrangements between the oil companies and their subsidiaries in Mozambique and South Africa. Initially supplies went by road over Beit Bridge; between February 1966 and March 1967 oil products were carried by rail from South Africa to Rhodesia via Mozambique; from 1967 to 1975 supplies went by rail, in bond, from Lourenço Marques to Rhodesia. Since then the new Rhodesia-South Africa direct rail link has been used.[40] The Bingham Report notes that at UDI "total consumption of all petroleum products in Rhodesia was running at an annual rate of about 410,000 tons. The total fell after UDI but was restored to the old level by about 1969 and thereafter increased until it now stands at about 800,000 tons."[41] The Report also note that the British government was aware of the scale of supply to Rhodesia as early as May 1966 and attempted to check it, but the non-co-operation of South Africa and Portugal made this impossible, unless an embargo on oil supplies to South Africa and Mozambique were also imposed. The British government concentrated its attention "on achieving a position in which it could truly be said that British companies were not engaged in supplying Rhodesia and that no British oil was reaching Rhodesia."[42] But the Beira blocade was not extended to Lourenço Marques.

Foreign trade was also maintained in other commodities, although with difficulty and at increased cost. From the time it was set up in 1968, the Security Council Sanctions Committee complained of the difficulty of determining the true origin of goods suspected as being 'Rhodesian' but carrying documentation certifying export from other sources. It proved equally difficult to determine whether Rhodesia was the ultimate destination of goods legally exported to the South African Customs Union (or to Portugal and Mozambique before the mid-1970s). Two motor assembly plants in Rhodesia which closed down following the imposition of sanctions had reopened by 1968, using imported kits; spare parts for vehicles and aircraft could be obtained at a price; and in 1973 three Boeing 707 model 720 jets reached Rhodesia after a complicated series of transactions which the Security Council Sanctions Committee tried to unravel.[43]

Most of the cases handled by the Sanctions Committee prior to 1973 were reported by Britain, and the majority of prosecutions for sanctions breaking have been in Britain and the US. Since 1973, information from non-governmental bodies, particularly the London *Sunday Times* and various church groups, enabled the Committee to expose an air link between Rhodesia and Europe using Gabon as a staging post[44] and various other illegal operations, but clearly the extent of the Committee's information is limited and governments are often reluctant to follow up Committee allegations.[45]

It is clear that sanctions had a direct and generally adverse impact on Rhodesian economic life, particularly on its export trade, but that this impact was limited and tolerable at a price. To the extent that sanctions stimulated industrial and agricultural diversification they might be viewed as useful. After thorough analysis Strack concluded that sanctions had not caused "*sustained* economic stagnation or recession", although they had imposed direct strains in the form of unfavourable terms of trade and an inability to obtain foreign capital on a large-scale; nor did he rule out further modest growth, in spite of sanctions.[46] Politically, the damaging effects of relegating the Rhodesian government and its supporters to a kind of international limbo were offset for a considerable time by the stiffened resolve of white Rhodesians to resist international pressure and go it alone. Their leaders reassured them that they could "tough it out" until things got better; but after 1975 they got worse. Since then Rhodesia has had to cope with the continuing strains imposed by sanctions and with a whole set of new problems – some shared by the rest of the world such as general recession, the deterioration in the terms of trade for primary products, and the inflationary spiral set in motion by oil price rises, and some of local relevance, such as the increased level of guerrilla warfare, congestion of South African railways and ports and a fall-off in white immigration combined with growing emigration rates.

Viewing the full range of economic restrictions in conjunction with the isolation of Rhodesia from the international community, not only by non-recognition of her independent status but in her exclusion from the multiplicity of international activities through conferences and meetings which are such a feature of our age, one must ascribe a cumulatively damaging effect to the overall UN programme. In the early years, the Smith regime hoped for a "withering away" of isolation; not only would economic sanctions break down (and here the Byrd amendment gave undue grounds for optimism) but international political acceptance would gradually come about. This proved a serious miscalculation of the calibre and tenacity of the forces ranged against Rhodesia which were to grow stronger not weaker in terms both of moral credibility and of the economic strength of many of the third world countries whose goodwill Britain and other western powers could not afford to forfeit. Over fifteen years, the UN norms of non-discrimination and majority rule progressively delegitimized the Rhodesian and South African concepts of white minority rule and apartheid. Sanctions against Rhodesia, while not bringing an immediate result, contributed to the process of undermining white rule there, and in the long run, probably in Southern Africa as a whole, but the guerrilla war, facilitated by the independence of Angola and Mozambique, and pressure from South Africa for a settlement were probably of greater significance.

Discussions at the Commonwealth Heads of Government meeting in Lusaka in August 1979 persuaded the British government to make a further effort to reconcile the Rhodesian government and the Patriotic Front on the basis of new constitutional proposals. At the time of writing the outcome of the London Conference is uncertain and South Africa has indicated that it would again give military aid to Rhodesia to avert a complete breakdown of law and order. It is clear that right-wing opinion in Britain and elsewhere in the West is in favour of lifting economic sanctions and recognizing the Muzorewa government. It remains to be seen whether this will come about; legally, mandatory sanctions can presumably only be lifted by the Security Council which imposed them. But in any event, UN sanctions would now seem to have less direct relevance for the future of Rhodesia than the other factors which have been discussed.

In the next two chapters a more detailed analysis of the problems faced by sanctionists and by targets of sanctions will provide opportunities for examining a number of interesting aspects of the Rhodesian case.

6 Problems of International Enforcement

In national societies, the state enjoys the legal monopoly of force and a recognized system of judicial process handles charges of law-breaking in the context of a published legal code. As a result, some may be deterred from breaking the law, while some of those who are not will be detected and prosecuted. But the incidence of success in detection, prosecution and conviction, even for petty offences, is obviously low and, as the record of implementation of US anti-trust legislation shows, there are immense difficulties in controlling corporate behaviour. Complicated and secret arrangements which circumvent or exploit loopholes in the law, skilful legal defence against charges of illegality, and vast resources which can be used without hardship to pay legal costs and fines, combine to render the law enforcement process uncertain at best against powerful corporate citizens. Coercing governments is not likely to be any easier and at the international level further problems are encountered. Members of the UN (or of other international bodies who seek to 'enforce' standards of behaviour) must play multiple roles as prosecutors, judges and law enforcement agencies, and must draw on their own resources in doing so. In the Charter, as noted in the previous chapter, the objective of Chapter VII was to provide for the effective enforcement of peace, failing other mechanisms of conciliation and mediation. Collective measures (i.e. sanctions) would penalize those deemed to have violated the Charter by threatening or breaking the peace. But the activation of this enforcement process by the Security Council, or by the competent organ of any international political organization seeking to discipline a member for breaking its rules, calls for a series of decisions taken collectively on the basis of consensus and individually within each national system. Several stages in this decision-making sequence can be noted. In the first place, a situation must be perceived and identified as one which requires collective action.

Secondly goals must be determined. Thirdly measures must be selected. Fourthly, these measures must be implemented, which may require each sanctioning state to promulgate regulations and orders, with penalties prescribed for their breach. Cost calculations will obviously be relevant for all participants and consensus will be crucial. This may be hard to achieve: not only are group decisions inherently more difficult to take and implement than individual decisions, but at the international level concerted action calls for harmonizing the policies of states of different sizes, strengths and ideologies, each jealous of its own sovereignty and prestige and pursuing distinct and possibly conflicting national goals.

A system of international enforcement might function success-fully in a genuinely international community with a cohesive social base where deviations from norms of accepted conduct were the exception rather than the rule. The weaker the system and the greater the diversity of values it contains, the more likely are doubts, hesitations and evasions. In the world today, the veto provisions of the Charter protect the permanent members from censure and the strength of the super-powers, who can threaten each other and the rest of the world with annihilation, makes penalties against them for non-compliance with international obligations non-enforceable in practical terms. Lesser powers are more vulnerable and sanctions potentially more damaging, but the risks of attracting them are minimized by the character of international society. Experience has shown that the determination of threats to or breaches of the peace, and decisions about action which should be taken to deal with them are not automatic even when minor powers are the culprits. Generally members of the UN have preferred to avoid or postpone decisions about enforcement because they do not agree on the question of culpability and because they are not prepared to bear the risks and costs which would accompany the imposition of penalties. Consensus on international sanctions is, therefore, elus-ive; in addition there are major problems of co-ordination as-sociated with any group operation. There may be scepticism about the behaviour of other members of the group; about the effectiveness of measures which might be adopted; about undesirable precedents which might be set; and about new power alignments which might be created. It is also hard to generate agreement on objec-tives.

THE PROBLEM OF GOAL-SETTING

Collective action which involves the commitment of national resources will be easier to organize if the overriding policy goals of a group of nations happen to coincide. This was true to a large extent of the Western Allies during World War II and of the West European recipients of Marshall Aid afterwards. In both cases, the best and vital interests of all members of the group were accepted as being served by co-operation and co-ordination of effort. In both a marked degree of harmony was achieved: in joint military operations under unified commands; in combined boards for allocation of supplies and in joint planning for the allocation of aid. Such occasions are rare and have been more typical of war than peace. Moreover, where value systems conflict sharply, even war-time alliances may bring little more than a formal and temporary association against a common enemy, with minimum co-ordination of effort and persistent underlying hostility. The alliance between the Soviet Union and the Western powers between 1941 and 1945 was of this nature. Much more common are cases when collective actions appears to conflict with national goals, is not obviously necessary for survival, and involves unwelcome sacrifice or hardship for the participants. Governments will then weigh the merits of action against inaction; they may question the grounds for action before a decision is made to embark on collective measures, and even when a decision has been made, they may have different sets of priorities and objectives in mind.

The objective of restoring peace, or of rectifying a situation which is deemed to threaten peace, would be achieved through sanctions if the offending state amended its policy as a result of their anticipated or felt impact. Threatened sanctions, to be effective, would create expectations of deprivation which would cancel out, or even outweigh the benefits which the target associates with the policy which is deemed offensive. If the deterrent effect of sanctions is not adequate, their imposition should bring compliance with the norms of behaviour required by the sanctionists. But the generalized definitions in international agreements of situations or circumstances in which sanctions of different types can be imposed, typically leave scope for widely varying perceptions by member states that such a situation or set of circumstances has arisen. Moreover the tactical decision to use a certain form of coercion will establish intermediate goals. If for instance, the final goal were the ending of hostilities between two states and the peaceful settlement of their dispute, and military measures were selected as appropriate means of coercion, then the intermediate goal would be to introduce an effective military presence into the area of hostilities, which would induce the delinquent state, or states, to abandon the use of force. On the other hand, if the ultimate goal of international action were to prevent a threatened act of aggression, and economic weapons were selected as instruments of coercion, then the intermediate goal would be to deprive the would-be aggressor of the means of waging war, or to make it too costly for him to do so. Moreover, as James Barber points out, the objectives of sanctionists may include the improvement of their own status as well as the correction or amelioration of the target state's behaviour.[1] And if the sanctioning process is protracted, the scope for divergence in objectives among and within the sanctioning states is greatly increased.

The grounds for imposing sanctions on Italy in 1935 were provided by her technical breach of the Covenant; her invasion of Ethiopia contravened obligations under Article 12 to refrain from the use of force at least for three months. If the sanctioning operation set in train under Article 16 had had a serious purpose, it would have been to check Italian aggression and prevent the conquest and annexation of Ethiopia. To accomplish this by economic measures, without resort to force by League members, it would have been necessary to make it impossible in terms of resources or too costly in terms of expenditure for Italy to continue her military campaign. However, the course of events in 1935 and 1936, which has been described in Chapter 4, compels the conclusion that the sanctions policy, at least in so far as Britain and France were concerned, was not designed to coerce Italy to any significant degree, but would be more accurately described as a face-saving exercise in half-hearted punishment, in which no more than the forms of the Covenant were observed. Although smaller League members hoped that sanctions would 'work' and thus demonstrate the value of the League system as a protection against aggression, the British and French governments of the day were following the ambivalent policy of making a gesture towards a fulfilment of international obligations while seeking to conciliate Mussolini in independent negotiations.

It has been noted that the conditions under which collective measures may be invoked under the Charter are very broadly defined. The extension of the enforcement powers of the Security Council to cover preventive as well as remedial action means that provided there is great power unanimity and adequate support from other members, the Council can designate any situation as a threat to the peace and require members to impose non-military measures against one or more states to deal with it. An overt act of aggression, or even a threat of external aggression, is not necessary. Moreover, provided that an existing situation is deemed to threaten the peace in terms of Article 39, the objective of sanctions may not be to preserve or restore the *status quo*, but to alter it.

This represents a considerable development of the whole concept of the use of international sanctions. It permits the Security Council to declare a situation is threatening the peace in order to defend norms of non-discrimination, majority rule and human rights, norms relevant to *internal* process and structure. Other international bodies such as the Commonwealth, the Council of Europe or the OAS may also seek to promote respect for human rights by recommending or imposing sanctions, and the United States in recent legislations has linked the granting of most-favoured-nation status to freedom of emigration, and the continuation of official development assistance to observance of minimum standards of human rights. Such attempts to influence the domestic policies of the target government will almost certainly be regarded by that government as improper intervention,[2] but even where an excellent case can be made for the propriety of the external pressure, as for instance in the case of Security Council decisions, the objective will be hard to realize. To bring about change in the internal political *structure* of another country is very ambitious. It offers scope for wide divergence of views among the sanctionists as to the extent and degree of change needed and increases possibilities of confusion and disagreement at all stages of the 'enforcement' process. If a peaceful outcome is sought, it also implies an eventual acceptance of the changed structure of their society by the nationals of the country concerned.

Over the past decade, African and Asian members of the United Nations have included the denial of human rights to Africans in Southern Africa among 'threats to the peace' and they have looked to the United Nations and other international organizations and associations as instruments of change which will hasten the objective of African majority rule over the whole of the African continent.

The anti-apartheid movement is a reflection of international consensus at an ethical level, but industrialized countries in the northern hemisphere have been reluctant to make material sacrifices in the cause of trying to bring change. The case for sanctions against South Africa has been argued forcibly on the grounds that failure to act will lead to exacerbation of tension in Southern Africa and race war. But the existence of a certain international consensus about the undesirability of racial discrimination does not extend to shared views about the appropriate international action, nor the appropriate alternative form of government for South Africa. The calling of a national convention representing all racial groups in the Republic and the introduction of a limited franchise for non-whites might go far to satisfy Western opinion, but it would not satisfy opinion in independent Africa. Within the Republic itself, African, Coloured, Indian, and white groups would have different aims, and there would be the danger of members of the United Nations identifying themselves with different groups and so adding to internal and international tensions and strains. If force is not to be used, and chaos is not to ensue, there would have to be a peaceful abdication of authority by the ruling group and an orderly transfer of power to other groups; in other words, a non-violent revolution. To achieve this by external economic coercion is a very tall order.

South Africa's decision to become a republic exposed her to Commonwealth expulsion; in the same manner, Rhodesia's unilateral declaration of independence ended British protection and exposed her to the full force of international condemnation. The Rhodesian case provides further illustration of the difficulties involved in defining and pursuing objectives of a political nature by collective economic action. Mandatory sanctions were imposed by the Security Council to meet a designated threat to the peace, but the technical consensus over the broad need to 'remove' this threat concealed a complex of attitudes and aspirations. Britain's primary aim was the restoration of legitimate constitutional government and *eventual* majority rule for African Rhodesians. Under these conditions the British government would have been prepared to initiate negotiations for the granting of formal independence. From the British government's point of view, the restoration of the constitutional *status quo ante* UDI would have been enough to justify the lifting of 'voluntary' sanctions in 1966, and this objective was still pursued in later negotiations, although it could not be regarded as a solution of the basic problem. But Britain herself did not have the motivation (or, perhaps, the capability) to impose a settlement; recourse to the United Nations appeared to be a means of sharing responsibility and of satisfying Commonwealth demands for action.

By 1968, Lord Thomson (then Secretary for Commonwealth Relations) saw sanctions as "a means of placing clearly before the Rhodesian community the choice between continuing with the rebellion and economic stagnation . . . and returning to legality and economic expansion".[3] This view was obviously shared by the British government. But the objectives of African states in supporting sanctions and calling for severer measures were more far-reaching and encompassed the elimination of white minority rule in Rhodesia. The years of complex and often fruitless diplomatic negotiations with the Smith regime bear witness to these difficulties.

When the government of Ian Smith finally accepted majority rule as a principle in 1977, and set up a transitional government with Bishop Muzorewa and Mr. Sithole as co-members, this "internal settlement" proved unacceptable to the Patriotic Front, its supporters in the Front-Line States and even to the British and American governments who were striving to bring about a transfer of power which would both avoid civil war and protect white interests.

The difficulty of ascribing or identifying collective goals, as distinct from the separate goals of participants in collective action is further illustrated by regional enforcement action undertaken by the OAS against Cuba. Not all members of the organization felt as strongly as the United States the need for drastic action against the Castro regime. Although Cuba was excluded from the inter-American system in January 1962, and an arms embargo was imposed at that time, sanctions in the form of severance of diplomatic and consular relations, a trade embargo, and a ban on shipping were not imposed until 1964, in spite of the missile crisis of October 1962. The goal of preventing the spread of revolutionary Communism in the hemisphere weighed more with Latin American countries than that of replacing the Castro regime with another.

Solidarity and consensus over goals have been characteristic of situations where an external enemy is perceived and identified. There will probably be little argument over the objectives of economic warfare among wartime allies but it was noticeable that differences of opinion in the West over the continuation and scope of strategic embargoes on trade with the Communist world became marked as cold war tension lessened in the mid-1950s, and as economic recovery permitted a more independent attitude on the part of West European governments.

The Arab states' identification of Israel as an enemy whose

continued existence must be challenged helps to maintain cohesion in their campaign of economic warfare. Internal pressures within Arab States and the claims of the Palestinians – which have been granted international recognition in the UN and many of its agencies – militate against concessions to Israel by any Arab leaders. The Arab bloc remained solid until President Sadat's peace initiative in November 1977 which was immediately denounced by militant Arab states who formed a "rejectionist front", and it is clear that Sadat's options are limited by the need for him to press the Palestinian cause. This more straightforward set of objectives enabled the Arab oil producers to design an effective strategy for their oil embargoes in 1973; its objective was to influence the *foreign policy* of target states and in this as we have seen, they achieved some successes.

Agreement on objectives may be elusive, but it is essential in a sanctioning process. Unless the competent sanctioning group is aware of what it wishes and needs to achieve by its policy, it will be unable to make rational choices between measures, to implement them effectively, or to know when they should be discontinued.

SELECTION OF MEASURES

Further problems are likely to arise over the selection of measures. A prescribed range of penalties to fit designated offences does not exist: the total boycott provisions of Article 16 of the Covenant were rapidly abandoned by League members in favour of selected and graduated penalties, while in the United Nations Charter it is left to the Security Council to impose any combination of measures thought appropriate. Economic sanctions can include some or all of the following: embargoes on financial and commercial dealings; restriction or severance of communications of all kinds; restrictions or prohibitions on the use of all types of transport. A ban on imports from the target state is intended to produce a shortage of foreign exchange and unemployment in export industries; a ban on exports to the target is intended to deprive it of essential commodities. Financial sanctions can deprive the target of access to foreign capital and money markets. Interference with communication can have serious economic effects, as well as producing a psychological sense of isolation. An extreme form of communications sanction would include physical blockade.

One would expect guidelines in choosing economic measures to be the possibility of general application of measures under consideration, their estimated effectiveness in relation to the circumstances of the delinquent state's economy, its sensitivity to external pressures and to the goals of the sanctionists and, finally, the minimization of cost and damage to the economies of the sanctionists themselves. In order to make these judgments, the target's economic structure and pattern of external economic relations would have to be studied in detail in order to determine specific areas of vulnerability, particularly the degree to which it is integrated into the world economy and its dependence on foreign trade, foreign investment, and other external services. Detailed analysis of national accounting statistics (presuming their availability) would show the nature and value of visible and invisible exports and imports; their contribution to the gross national product; the proportion of exports to re-exports; the extent to which imports were processed for export, and the importance of imports for the continuation of economic activity at its existing level. Probable effects on employment which might follow the loss of export markets could be calculated; the scope for expanding domestic production to bring about import substitution could be estimated. Multiplier effects of unemployment would have to be taken into account, and the resulting falls in income levels estimated, although the number of variables would make precise quantification difficult.

Estimates of the effects of cutting off external aid, recourse to foreign capital markets, and other financial services would require a study of the development plans and potential of the target, the level of domestic savings, possibilities of economy in public spending, and other related factors.

Certain other difficulties make assessment of the effects of particular sanctions even less reliable. The time factor would be all important: how soon the sanctions would take effect is a different problem from that of how soon they could be put into effect. It takes time for the full effects of economic restraints to work their way through an economy, and much depends on the capacity of the target to adapt to the new situation. Furthermore, it is impossible to calculate with any degree of precision the probable reaction of individuals or groups in a target state to externally induced falls in income levels. There may be an unforseen willingness to accept a measure of sacrifice, and falls in real income produced by sanctions may not be sufficient either to persuade the government of the target, under pressure from its citizens, to change its policy, or to bring an alternative government into power. The situation becomes less calculable if the change in policy desired by members of the international organization would itself bring, or would be expected to bring, lower incomes or a fall in the standard of living of politically influential sectors of the population, an aspect of sanctions particularly relevant to the Rhodesian case as will be seen in the next chapter.

States having predominantly agricultural economies and industrialized states not dependent on outside sources of supply or markets will obviously be less vulnerable to economic sanctions than those whose external relationships are crucial to their economic life. It is also clear that some states are more vulnerable than others to pressure designed to achieve a specific goal. For instance, aggression by a small country which had no domestic armaments industry and which depended on a single crop for its export earnings, could, in theory, be speedily checked by a general embargo on the supply of arms and ammunition, supplemented by a ban on imports into other countries of its export staple. A major industrial power with aggressive intentions would need to be subjected to a much more elaborate system of economic restraints unless perhaps it were heavily dependent on imported energy supplies which could readily be cut off.

The experience of the Arab oil embargo in 1973–74 confirms that countries like Japan, South Africa and Israel who are heavily dependent on imports of oil, would be in serious difficulties if an effective embargo were imposed. It is now known that Rhodesia continued to receive oil via South Africa through swap arrangements made by the oil majors; otherwise the Smith regime might have fulfilled Harold Wilson's prediction and collapsed in a matter of weeks. Israel has a US promise of supply on which to rely; Japan will obviously ensure that friendly relations are maintained with oil producers. But South Africa which at present imports 99 per cent of its oil, and which will still need to import 88 per cent after 1981 when SASOL II, its second oil from coal plant comes into production, is more vulnerable. Its isolated position in the international community could make it more difficult to break or evade a full-scale embargo. The South African government's attempts to reduce this dependence and cushion the effects of an embargo are discussed in the next chapter.

Decisions to select certain measures and to reject others give scope for individual sanctionist states to plead their own cases in respect of restrictions which would affect their domestic trade, balance of payments, or communications unduly, while partial or selective sanctions also permit exemptions and exceptions which may assume major proportions. This tendency needs to be restrained: an authority on the League's only sanctioning experiment commented aptly that 'the acid of exemptions will eat the very heart out of the sanctions system.'[4]

SCOPE OF SANCTIONS

The universal application of selective sanctions, if they were judiciously chosen, would achieve maximum effectiveness within the limits of the international programme. This represents the ideal rather than the attainable situation. It is unrealistic to envisage all countries, whether members of the United Nations or not, co-operating fully in imposing a total boycott on economic relations with a delinquent state. This was the picture painted by Article 16 of the League Covenant, picturesquely described as a "revival of medieval excommunication".[5] In the attempts which have been made by organizations at the universal level to maintain 'peace' by the use of economic sanctions, no more than partial application has been achieved, while sanctioning at the regional level is obviously subject to limitations.

Without universality of application, vulnerability to external economic pressure is drastically lessened. The existence of non-participants in enforcement brings possibilities of important trading relationships being left untouched by sanctions; of alternative markets and sources of supply becoming available; of evasive action being channelled through third states; of loans, credits, and even gifts from friendly powers; and the development of new communications and lines of transport to replace those cut by sanctions. The psychological effect of the sanctions policy will also be weakened.

In cases of limited application of sanctions, considerations of cost and minimum disruption of trade may encourage emphasis on import embargoes. Sanctionists will be less enthusiastic about export embargoes because the target may be able to obtain its requirements from other sources and the loss of markets for sanctionists may be permanent.

In deciding on a blockade, or on other controls which will limit the target's ability to obtain help from third states, the sanctionists' own relations with these states will come under close scrutiny. Blockade is costly and may involve confrontation leading to violence; disruption of economic relations with a group of states will be even less welcome than sanctions on a single target.

The United States used the threat of withholding economic and technical aid to induce observance of embargoes on trade with the Communist bloc by West European countries, and the Arab League has made considerable use of blacklisting to strengthen and extend the scope of its boycott of Israel. These policies were conceived as being in the interests of national security; international sanctions for non-observance of a sanctions policy are likely to be less powerfully motivated and thus less readily imposed.

Neither the League nor the United Nations has dealt successfully with this problem of secondary enforcement. The League, with its limited membership, was hampered throughout its life because major trading nations, particularly the United States were in a position to supply the essential needs of any target of sanctions, thereby making the economic weapon more than usually blunt.[6] Moreover Germany and Japan, after leaving the League in the 1930s, were not likely to be cooperative.

The problem of non-members is one aspect of the limitations of international enforcement facing members of an international organization; the other is the problem of members who do not participate. In the Italian case, several League members refrained from participating, leaving a wide gap in the sanctions front. Austria, Albania, and Hungary were the chief offenders and their proximity to Italy made their defection a serious matter. A proposal was made to reduce imports from non-participating states to the extent to which they benefited from sanctions, but it was not implemented.

When the revision of the Covenant was being discussed after the failure of this sanctions experiment, the Sovient Union proposed that any member who failed to participate in economic and financial sanctions should be subjected to measures of customs and trade discrimination on the part of member states. This logical suggestion was not acted upon and it would have been difficult to implement if a number of states were in the category of non-participants.

The Charter sought to overcome the problem by providing that

UN members must comply with Security Council decisions. Although the UN has achieved near universality of membership, failure to observe the obligations imposed by the Charter does not automatically lead to the imposition of any penalty; the logical outcome would be the extension of sanctions to the defaulting or 'accessory' members, but this would involve further cost and dislocation of trade for the sanctionists. Moreover, *recommendations* of the Assembly – or the Security Council – leave room for non-compliance by members.

The measures selected as sanctions against Rhodesia were more comprehensive than those imposed on Italy by the League in 1935, but they were not made total until May 1968. The selective nature of sanctions from December 1966 to May 1968 however, was probably less important than the partial scope of their application. Non-members of the United Nations were not sympathetic to the illegal regime, but Switzerland adopted a neutral stance and permitted limited trade.[7] Two members, South Africa and Portugal, played a crucial role in helping Rhodesia to survive. Portugal queried the legality of the Security Council resolution, arguing that Rhodesia fell within Britain's domestic jursidiction, and requested compensation for loss of revenue in Mozambique due to sanctions, particularly the blockade of Beira. The South African government declared on the day of UDI that its policy was one of non-involvement and maintenance of trade with Rhodesia at normal levels. Dr. Verwoerd is reported to have stated that South Africa was not the weak link in the chain of sanctions; it was not a link at all. Moreover normal trade could mean expanding trade under conditions of competition.[8] After UN sanctions were imposed, the South African government ignored all inquiries from the United Nations about its trade with Rhodesia. It did not recognize the independence of Rhodesia *de jure*; but *de facto* and close relations were maintained with the Rhodesian government. Both Portugal and South Africa probably felt confident that in defying the United Nations they would not bring retribution on their own heads: it is no secret that Britain was not prepared to sponsor punitive measures against them.

The Portuguese situation changed after the fall of Salazar and the independence of Angola and Mozambique, but South Africa has continued to give economic assistance to the Rhodesian regime. Moreover, it is now clear that UN sanctions, particularly the oil sanction, have been evaded from the very early days. The revelations of the Bingham Report and other documentation described in the previous chapter show that oil swap arrangements between British and French oil companies made it possible for Rhodesia to obtain oil via South Africa; the Beira blockade by British naval patrols was a farce at the British taxpayer's expense. In addition to this glaring gap in the sanctions programme, circuitious means of exporting and importing have been in use throughout the period. Moreover, for several years the US openly imported chrome, nickel and other materials from Rhodesia in violation of its obligations under the UN Charter; and the submission by the US government of voluntary reports on the quantities involved, the flag of the vessels used for transportation and the ports of loading and unloading, which enabled the Sanctions Committee to investigate cases where vessels of non-US registration were involved, seems inconsequential in the context of US policy.

The limitations of programmes of economic denial which – however comprehensive – are applied by regional groupings of states but not backed by force are illustrated by the experience of the OAS in the Western hemisphere. When embargoes were imposed on Cuba by the United States and the OAS, the United States was Cuba's leading trading partner. But Cuba proceeded to draw material and ideological support from the Soviet Union which assumed a dominant role in Cuban economic life and assisted the regime of Fidel Castro to continue its new programme of economic and social development. The experience of China, Yugoslavia and Albania in re-orienting their economic relationships under Soviet pressure is further evidence of the importance of third-party support.

THE COST FACTOR

No international enforcement action involving sanctions of a military or economic nature can possibly be undertaken without some cost and in selecting measures the need to minimize costs to the economies of the sanctionist groups is more likely to be stressed than overlooked. The smaller and more insignificant the object of sanctions, the less disruption will be caused by a ban on economic intercourse; a major industrial country which is not considered to be observing its international obligations will present a harder set of choices to would-be sanctionists. Compensation for any participant who is particularly hard hit would seem to be a logical corollary to a sanctions policy, and a means of discouraging evasion and partial implementation. But even a small target which is subjected to economic sanctions may mean difficulties for its neighbours and a distortion of the natural economic development of the region.

Apart from the special problem of assisting a state which is under attack, there is the general problem of sharing costs of enforcement between the sanctionists. Economic relationships are multi-directional, and the impact on the target of cutting trade or other links may be equalled on the sanctionist side, although it will be spread over a number of states. It will not, however be evenly spread, and certain of the sanctionists may be particularly vulnerable to the interruption of trade – or to counter-sanctions. It is hardly fair to expect this burden to be borne wholly by the state in question, when other – and possibly richer – states are not affected adversely or to the same degree. In the case of military measures, contributions to a collective effort can be directly linked to capacity, but economic measures may place a disproportionate burden on those who are least able to carry it. Costs can be spread through compensatory arrangements; alternatively, certain states may be excused full implementation. Failing this, there will be a disposition to non-implementation or even defection from the sanctionist front.

Opposition to sanctions can be expected from groups within each country who will bear the brunt of their costs. The effect of national embargoes on specific producers and traders could be severe, even if external trade were only to account for a small fraction of the gross national product. In a major trading nation powerful pressure groups may be affected. Resentment at loss of trade may be deeply felt; instead of war, which may mean profits, sanctions may simply mean sacrifice and loss in a poorly comprehended cause. 'Aggressive' behaviour may be displayed by both parties to a dispute, making the attribution of guilt as a basis for sanctions more complicated; and if the grounds for collective action involve the internal 'reform' of foreign societies, not the checking of external, visible aggression, the issues will be even more confused.

In democratic countries where governments must retain the support of the electorate, it will be necessary to explain and justify the domestic effects of the imposition of sanctions – or risk being defeated at the polls. In a pre-election period, or when a minority government is precariously balanced, decisions to vote for international sanctions may be weighed even more carefully than at other times. After the November 1935 election in Britain, which was fought largely on the issue of support for sanctions and the League, the government was well placed to take firm action, though it did not do so. Similarly, the Labour government of Mr. Wilson was better able to take steps to deal with the Rhodesian situation after the general election of April 1966, when it gained a substantial majority, than at the time of UDI in November 1965 when its majority in the House of Commons was three.

Attempts by domestic interests to frustrate embargoes are likely to continue after sanctions have been imposed, particularly if powerful interest groups are unconvinced of the merits of, or necessity for a sanctions policy. A stable though repressive regime in South Africa may offer considerable economic advantages to certain groups in other countries who are less concerned about the equity of the political system or who doubt that sanctions can be effective as instruments of reform. There may be attempts to curb sanctions-breaking activities by severe penalties within sanctionist states, or they may go unchecked. To the inevitable backlash effect of sanctions, must be added the effect of counter-sanctions. The combination of the two can mean that production and employment in export industries fall off, while the multiplier effect will transmit the shrinkage to other sectors of the economy. A cessation of imports from the usual supplies may mean that goods have to be obtained from alternative sources at a higher price, leading to cost inflation and possible balance of payments strain.

In periods of national or international economic stress, recourse to sanctions which distort trade patterns and lead to a loss of export markets will be a particularly unattractive prospect. The League Covenant in Article 16(3) stated that members would support one another in financial and economic measures taken under that article "in order to minimize the loss and inconvenience" resulting from them and "in resisting any special measures aimed at one of their number by the Covenant-breaking State". At the time of the Italo-Ethiopian dispute, the world had not recovered from the Depression and there were still serious unemployment problems in industrial countries. International trade was shrinking as a result of policies of economic nationalism and it was an unpropitious moment to forgo economic advantage. In the Italo-Ethiopian crisis no help of any kind was given to Ethiopia by the League. She had been subject to an arms embargo for some months prior to the

Italian invasion, which made it impossible for her to obtain military supplies and equipment, and although this embargo was lifted after the commencement of hostilities, it was then too late for her to build up her defences. Moreover her financial resources were limited, and her appeals for financial assistance were ignored.[9] Assuming that a sanctions policy, even if limited to economic measures, is intended to be of practical value in restoring peace, the failure to assist a victim of unprovoked aggression who, as in this case, could be readily identified, is a serious weakness. Moreover, states which applied sanctions and suffered a consequent loss of trade received little help from other League members. Members who refused to apply sanctions, on grounds that they would cause economic hardship, such as Albania, Austria and Hungary, thus fared better than Yugoslavia who supported League policy and suffered considerable loss. One-fifth of her exports normally went to Italy and much of that trade was lost. The sole effort made by League members to deal with the problem was to guarantee that most-favoured-nation treatment would not be forfeited by states which ceased to trade with Italy. Exhortations for the replacement of imports from Italy with imports from other sanctionists, and for negotiations to offset losses were of no practical effect. The lesson was not lost; in discussions of League reform Switzerland pointed out that for a small country, the application of Article 16 might be a matter of life or death. When Finland appealed for help under Articles 11 and 16 of the Covenant, following the Soviet attack in 1939, plans for despatch of military and non-military supplies were drawn up but came to nothing because rights of passage were refused by other Scandinavian countries.

Discussions at the United Nations on the subject of sanctions against South Africa have produced specific objections from the Republic's major trading partners that such action would have serious disruptive effects on their own economies and would entail considerable losses of trade and external earnings, while economic sanctions against Rhodesia have inevitably brought some losses to sanctionists in the form of trade forgone, and direct costs in payments of aid. For instance, in 1965 British exports to Rhodesia were worth £31.7 million. Under sanctions they were virtually eliminated.

Serious problems have also been encountered by Rhodesia's neighbours and they have invoked Article 50 of the Charter which provides that any member or non-member which "finds itself confronted with special economic problems arising from the carrying out" of preventive or enforcement measures "shall have the right to consult the Security Council with regard to a solution of these problems".

The burden on the Front Line States

From the outset, Zambia discounted the efficacy of economic measures against Rhodesia and advocated the use of force. As neighbouring states and until 1965 co-partners with Malawi in the Federation of Rhodesia and Nyasaland, the economies of the two countries were closely linked, and sanctions against Rhodesia would obviously be damaging to Zambia. Botswana, Tanzania and post-independence Mozambique have also found themselves in the 'front line' as a result of economic sanctions against Rhodesia and through their support for guerrilla movements seeking to overthrow the Rhodesian regime by force.

The UN has responded to a limited degree with assistance for Zambia, Botswana and Mozambique. The Commonwealth, too, has given help to these states, including Mozambique which is not a member of the Commonwealth. A study prepared for the Commonwealth Secretariat in 1978 includes among the costs and effects of the struggle to end minority rule in Namibia, Rhodesia and South Africa "the need to develop alternative strategies to relieve the previous dependence on the minority regimes, the inability under present circumstances to plan optimal development policies for the Southern African region as a whole in such fields as communications, river control and energy development; the additional cost of security and the burden of refugees".[10]

Zambia has been particularly hard hit; being generally oriented southwards to Rhodesia, Mozambique and South Africa. The copper mines which were the mainstay of the economy (providing over 90 per cent of foreign earnings) depended on Rhodesian coal which was carried by Rhodesian railways; the same railways carried copper to the coast for shipment and provided Zambia's main transport link with the outside world. Rail and air services were jointly owned and operated until June 1967; the Beira-Umtali pipeline served both countries; the jointly owned Kariba hydro-electric project was situated in Rhodesia. Furthermore, Zambia was accustomed to importing about one-third of her total imports from

Rhodesia and 94 per cent from Rhodesia and South Africa together. Alternative road transportation routes were unsatisfactory, and the Benguela railway was closed in 1975 during the Angolan civil war. This meant that the border with Rhodesia, closed in 1973,[11] would have had to be reopened if the pipeline to Dar-es-Salaam and the Tazara railway, linking the copperbelt with Dar and built with Chinese aid had not been completed.[12] As it is, the railway line is over-burdened and Dar-es-Salaam is choked with shipping; Zambia was forced to reopen the border for rail traffic through Rhodesia in 1978 or face a total collapse of the economy, and serious congestion in transportation is still causing major problems.

Problems were compounded by the dramatic fall in copper prices between 1974 and 1975, which cannot be attributed to sanctions or the liberation struggle, but other strains are clearly the direct result of attempts to develop self-sufficiency, (e.g. hydro-electric projects) and to diversify trade which has meant higher priced imports as well as new transport routes. The Commonwealth Secretariat report notes that not only are some of these enterprises likely to be redundant when a peaceful settlement is achieved, but also that local and foreign investment have declined because political and economic uncertainties militate against risk-taking.[13] Per capita national income in Zambia has decreased.

Tanzania has been less seriously affected but the provision of transport facilities for Zambia constitutes a continuing burden; Botswana has been rendered more dependent on South Africa (as indeed have Zambia and Mozambique). Mozambique which closed the border with Rhodesia and imposed sanctions in March 1976 has lost foreign exchange and jobs as a result, and resources which were needed for reconstruction after the liberation struggle have had to be diverted to other purposes.

These costs cannot be separated from the costs of supporting guerrilla bases and refugees – who have become more numerous since the forces of the Patriotic Front began to make serious incursions into Rhodesian territory. And the collapse of copper prices is not a consequence of sanctions. But some estimates of the cost of sanctions in the early stages of the programme have been made; the former Co-ordinator of UN assistance to Zambia, Sir Robert Jackson, attributed $100 million expenditure to the consequence of UDI and the decision to apply sanctions in the period 1965–68.[14] In the next three years 1969–72, at least an equivalent amount was spent; between 1972–1977 (which covers the border closure with Rhodesia in 1973) $744 million. Estimates of cost to Mozambique of applying sanctions have also been made by UN Missions. In the first year 1975–76, direct costs were put at between $139–$165 million and thereafter about $110–$135 million per annum.[15] Losses stemmed from earnings of migrant workers, substitutes for Rhodesian facilities and an increased trade deficit. In fact Mozambique needed and will continue to need balance of payments support for several years. As of April 1977 $102 million had been offered from external sources to offset the effects of sanctions.[16]

Economic sanctions against Rhodesia have placed a heavy burden on these struggling economies, which already faced appalling problems of underdevelopment, illiteracy, lack of industrial base and public services, not to mention the incidence of natural disasters such as floods and droughts. And while it is true that their support for the armed struggle in Rhodesia has increased this burden, violence was not their chosen instrument for change. The Lusaka Manifesto, adopted in 1969, put peaceful methods first. It is clear that comprehensive sanctions which dislocate existing patterns of economic activity can bear as heavily on innocent neighbours as on the delinquent target; if South Africa were to be subjected to international sanctions, the neighbouring states of Central and Southern Africa would inevitably suffer adverse consequences which could only be partially offset by UN or Commonwealth aid.

POLICING AND SUPERVISING SANCTIONS

Effective implementation of a programme of international economic sanctions calls for co-ordination of effort, for effective national control systems which ensure that embargoed goods do not slip through the sanctions net and perhaps for international supervisory mechanisms. During the Second World War, the Allied economic effort was closely coordinated, and liaison maintained between government departments in Britain and the United States. An expert intelligence service was built up which sifted information collected from all parts of the world, and provided data for the efficient application of controls and restrictions to neutral trade. Similarly, in the postwar period, Western embargoes on trade with the Communist bloc were co-ordinated by the two standing committees, COCOM and CHINCOM, appointed by the Consultative Group on which all participants were represented. The Communist boycott of Yugoslavia was probably co-ordinated by COMECON under Soviet leadership, and the Arab League maintains a Central Boycott Office in Damascus to plan and implement its campaign of economic warfare against Israel.

Nothing on a comparable scale has been attempted either by the League or the United Nations. The Covenant provided no guidance on the mechanics of enforcement and procedures had to be devised on an *ad hoc* basis to co-ordinate and supervise the application of sanctions against Italy.[17]

League sanctions were agreed in principle on 10 October 1935 and members accepted 19 November as the date on which the agreed measures would come into effect. In view of the unprecedented and *ad hoc* nature of the operation, this was perhaps not an undue delay, although the embargo on imports did not take full effect until January 1936. Delays resulted from the failure of governments to make legislative provision for the rapid application of sanctions; only Czechoslovakia had organized statutory implementation of Article 16 before 1935. As a result of the crisis, some governments enacted special legislation which generally had relevance only to this one case.

The first step in organizing the implementation of the sanctions policy was to set up a general co-ordinating committee which included all members of the League. In turn, this body appointed a Committee of Eighteen which was responsible for proposing specific measures, collating government responses to proposals, maintaining liaison with non-members, and dealing with other relevant matters. Its work was handled by three main sub-committees which dealt with economic measures, financial measures, and mutual support. There were also committees of legal and military experts. Replies from governments regarding the various proposals were classified according to intentions regarding participation, and comments were made on the content of national legislation. Doubts about the scope and interpretation of such legislation were clarified with the governments themselves, sometimes by oral examination of their representatives.

In December 1935 a special Committee of Experts made a report to the Committee of Eighteen on the position regarding sanctions, and this report was passed to the Co-ordinating Committee. By this time, however, the impetus had gone out of the sanctions policy and the Co-ordinating Committee did not meet again formally until the termination of sanctions in July 1936. Nevertheless, in January 1936 the Committee of Eighteen instructed the Experts Committee to collect information on trade between Italy and the sanctioning group. A simple questionnaire was drawn up to provide empirical data about imports and exports on a monthly basis, which would be helpful in evaluating the effects of the sanctions programme. A report was also made by a special committee on the feasibility of imposing an oil sanction, but no further action was taken until the Co-ordinating Committee met in July to recommend the lifting of sanctions. A comment by a distinguished one-time member of the Committee of Eighteen is revealing: Lester B. Pearson described its work as a "mockery, for it was used by Pierre Laval, and others, as a committee to sabotage and not enforce sanctions".[18]

In seeking to ensure that sanctions were observed, League members had to rely on the exercise of control at source of exports to Italy and on checks carried out at destination on imports suspected of originating in Italy. There was no physical blockade and it was not always possible to control the ultimate destination of exports or to verify the true source of imports. The arms embargo which was largely of symbolic significance, proved to be the easiest of the embargoes to administer: it involved no more than the inclusion of prohibited items in existing licensing systems. Other export embargoes on transport animals, rubber, and minerals were enforced by order or decree in sanctionist countries and the checking of consignments was carried out by customs officials. The import embargoes proved much more difficult to administer and enforce. Problems arose over the identification of Italian goods coming from third countries, particularly agricultural products, and over the question of whether goods were exempt from the embargoes either because they were in transit by 18 November 1935, or had been wholly paid for by 18 October. Resultant delays worked in Italy's favour. Further difficulties arose from the value-added exemption: goods sent outside Italy for processing were exempt from embargo if at least 25 per cent were subsequently added to their value. The non-participation of Italy's neighbours in the sanctions policy obviously compounded all these difficulties.

Many of the problems described above have recurred in United Nations experience over Rhodesia, in spite of the fact that the organization and implementation of measures was expected to be simpler and more effective because of the concentration of authority in the hands of the Security Council. In fact, the first serious appraisal of general procedures relating to the application of UN economic sanctions was undertaken not by a Security Council Committee, but by the Collective Measures Committee, set up by the General Assembly in terms of the Uniting for Peace Resolution in 1950. The Committee's recommendations made in three reports,[19] remained a dead letter. Among them was a proposal for the establishment of a co-ordinating committee which would be in continuous session and would plan, evaluate, and supervise the application of collective measures.

The Additional Measures Committee set up to handle the co-ordination of economic measures against North Korea and China in 1951 was given no executive power. The responsibility for determining commodities to be embargoed and specific forms of control was left to the individual states, who were to report to the committee. In turn, it was to comment on the effectiveness of the embargo and the desirability of continuing, extending, or relaxing it. It did not carry out these duties and ceased to meet once negotiations for an armistice had started.

Reference has already been made in Chapter 5 to the Security Council Committee which in the mid-1960s was given the specific task of studying the feasibility of applying economic sanctions to South Africa; the problem became more than academic with the decision in 1966 to apply sanctions to Rhodesia.

In the initial phase of the Rhodesia sanctions policy, there was no inter-governmental co-ordination of action at the United Nations. A Commonwealth Sanctions Committee was set up following the Prime Ministers' Conference in Lagos in January 1966; regular meetings are held in London, attended by High Commissioners and a British government representative of ministerial rank. Meetings are held in secret and minutes are not published. The function of this committee (renamed the Commonwealth Committee on Southern Africa in 1976) is to maintain surveillance over trade with Rhodesia and to attempt to check sanctions evasion by making representations to governments. It relies heavily on information gathered by the Commonwealth Secretariat.

There were delays in the application of Commonwealth measures following UDI: the British embargo on all exports to Rhodesia did not take effect until the end of January 1966. Similarly, the United Nations sanctions ordered by Resolution 232 in December 1966 did not take immediate effect. Some time lags resulted from the legislative non-competence of those members who had not taken to heart the recommendations of the Collective Measures Committee regarding legislative preparedness.[20]

When mandatory sanctions were first imposed, the Secretary-General was requested to report at regular intervals on implementation by members. In January 1967 an official request was sent to all governments asking for monthly returns of information and using a standard form of questionnaire; a series of reports to the Security Council summarized the information collected by this means. It was left to each member to devise its own mode of implementation, with no standardized controls or exemption procedures, and no independent system of inspection. In May 1968, as a result of the adoption of Resolution 253, the range of restrictions was made far more comprehensive and a Security Council Sanctions Committee was established, with the duty of examining reports from the Secretariat, and of seeking information from members about implementation of sanctions and possible sanctions-breaking activities.[21] There were originally seven members of this committee, four permanent members of the Security Council (Britain, France, the US and USSR) and three non-permanent, but in 1970 it was enlarged to fifteen to include all Security Council members. It holds regular meetings in closed session and operates by consensus. A chairman is elected annually. The Committee receives reports of alleged sanctions-violations from governments (virtually all from the British government) and, (since 1973) from individuals and non-governmental bodies.[22] It proceeds to investigate by seeking information from governments. The Secretariat provides data and statistical material to assist the Committee in its work and a no-objection procedure has been developed whereby the Secretariat attaches a draft reply or suggested course of action to the text of communications received. If no member of the Committee objects, this action is taken; otherwise there is a discussion at a meeting.

The Committee has received an average of 50 new cases each year and many continue under investigation over a long period. In 1977, 342 cases were under consideration. Governments are slow to reply to inquiries and the network of links operating to handle illegal trade with Rhodesia is often incredibly complex and hard to expose. A system of reminders has been instituted and if governments do not reply to Committee inquiries their names are eventually published in a press release. Personal contacts are sought by the Chairman with representatives of governments who have not replied after three reminders or at the specific request of the Committee.[23] But replies may be quite perfunctory and non-enlightening and apart from a few important cases which were initially brought to light through the detective-work of investigative journalists, the cases dealt with by the Committee represent no more than the tip of the iceberg of sanctions-evasion. A manual of documentation and procedures to assist governments in detecting and dealing with sanctions violations has been under consideration for some years, but delegates to the Committee change and it is noted in the 1977 report that its consideration had (again) been deferred because new delegates had not had time to study it and because of its "highly technical nature".[24]

The Committee considers general issues as well as specific cases; in 1976 it decided to adopt a formula by which it would devote four meetings in a row to the latter, and then two to the former. Examples of general issues are relations with the OAU, closer contacts with non-governmental bodies, and the expansion of sanctions. There is a continuing division of opinion in the Committee between the USSR and third world representatives on the one hand and western representatives on the other in respect of the propriety of forwarding a recommendation to the Security Council for the extension of sanctions to South Africa. Britain and the US see this as outside the Committee's terms of reference.[25]

In recent years the Committee has focussed its attention on sports events involving Rhodesians particularly those "of a representative nature" where individuals or groups were acting in a nationally representative capacity.[26] It is true that such events might involve the transfer of funds or the entry into member countries of Rhodesian passport-holders and thus violate Security Council Resolution 253, but the principal objective is obviously to increase the psychic isolation of Rhodesians – a form of boycott which has also been applied to South Africans under Commonwealth auspices.[27]

The main weapon of the Security Council Committee is that of publicity; it is powerless to follow up instances of sanctions-breaking except by urging governments to do so within their national jurisdictions. That its zeal has occasionally outrun its good sense is illustrated by the remarks made by the Zambian government representative who appeared before the Committee at her own request on 28 July, 1977.[28] She pointed out that as a 'front line' state, Zambia was active in opposition to the Rhodesian regime and was therefore unhappy to find itself listed in a press release as not replying to Committee inquiries, which suggested a lack of enthusiasm in following up cases of sanctions breaking. She then referred to the *Tango Romeo* case which involved an airfreight service from Rhodesia to Europe via Gabon, noting that overflight of Zambian air space by Rhodesian planes was forbidden. With a nice touch of irony, she pointed out that "the Committee was probably already aware that the Zambian authorities could know about flights over their territory only if they were informed of them in advance", an unlikely contingency in this and similar cases, and that as a large and relatively undeveloped country, Zambia could not "monitor every inch of its air space". Thirdly, she noted that, in a case relating to tobacco off-loaded at Alexandria, Zambia has no control over commodities once they had been sold and consigned outside Zambia. Her final point is of general interest and quite pertinent; that ". . . cases referred to dated back to 1973 and were somewhat out of date . . . the Committee should pay greater attention to the many current violations of sanctions, some of which such as the role of the Western oil companies in supporting the Smith regime were extremely serious. The Committee should resist any attempts . . . to divert its attention from actual and serious breaches of sanctions to what might really be extraneous cases, especially if it wished to retain its credibility . . ."[29]

Within national administrations, it is clear that surveillance of sanctions-breaking by private business interests is not a high priority and the British government's assiduous reporting of suspected violations to the UN Sanctions Committee, as well as its record of prosecuting some sanctions violators within its own area of jurisdiction looks a great deal less impressive in the light of the disclosures officially confirmed by the Bingham Report that senior ministers knew from early in 1968 that oil was reaching Rhodesia through a chain of suppliers which included subsidiaries of BP and Shell.[30] In his study of the Dutch government's efforts to carry out its undertaking for full implementation of sanctions, P. J. Kuyper reveals the legal and practical difficulties which arose within and between bureaucratic and business sectors in the Netherlands.[31]

This chapter has examined some of the major organizational problems associated with framing and implementing a programme of international economic sanctions. In the next chapter, the reaction and strategies of the target state will be subjected to scrutiny.

7 Reaction to Sanctions

The most economical use of sanctions would be the case where the threat was sufficient to induce the target to alter its policy and comply with the demands of the sanctionists; once sanctions are imposed, speedy compliance would minimize cost and dislocation. But in all cases of sanctioning examined in this study, the response of the target state has been negative; there has been rejection of the authority of the sanctioning group and a determined effort to resist, circumvent and overcome the effects of economic deprivation. Successful defiance of sanctions may vindicate this stand; it may also produce durable, and possibly beneficial changes in the structure of the target's economy, alter international economic relationships and establish new patterns of trading, and boost the cost of sanctions beyond the level expected by or acceptable to the sanctioning group. The fact that a sanctioning venture which appeared excessively costly to sanctionists would probably not be attempted in the first place does not make this point academic. There may well be a misperception of the defensive and counter-offensive strengths of the target, leading to miscalculation of the ease with which its policies can be externally influenced.

ANTICIPATORY ACTION

It has been pointed out that an international organization is unlikely to act speedily or 'out of the blue' in framing and implementing a programme of economic sanctions. In some cases, notably that of South Africa, sanctions may be considered over a period of years and opportunities for building up immunity are greatly enhanced. Even where decisions are taken fairly quickly, there is likely to be a short preliminary period in which the pros and cons are debated which will provide the target with an opportunity to take anticipatory action to minimize the effects of measures which may be imposed.

It would be as unrealistic to suggest that action could be taken to guarantee the failure of sanctions by all potential targets as to claim that all are vulnerable.[1] Self-sufficiency, economic strength and the capacity to reduce vulnerability are unequally distributed among states. Provided the government of a country remains in power, and its programme receives adequate support from the politically significant elements in the population, it will be able to plan effectively for a greater measure of self-sufficiency, even if this involves a sacrifice of some economic advantage.

Even in the Italian case, where it only became likely that sanctions would be applied a short time before League decisions were taken, Mussolini 'began to prepare the Italian people to meet them'.[2] Political and economic measures were instituted, including controls over foreign exchange, and an intensive propaganda campaign mounted. In the Second World War, Germany was much better prepared for conditions of partial siege than in the first, particularly through building up 'ersatz' industries and by bringing the Balkan countries under its economic hegemony.[3]

How far the government of a state threatened with sanctions will go in taking positive anticipatory action, as opposed to drawing up contingency plans, will depend on powers and resources, and on the credibility and intimidatory content of the threat. As Raymond Aron points out, any threat "is less convincing in proportion as its execution is contrary to the interests of those who make it".[4]

Rhodesia was warned in October 1964 that UDI would lead to British sanctions; all sectors of the economy thus had over a year to plan and strengthen their defences, while the Rhodesian government was able to time the declaration of independence to their best advantage.[5]

South Africa, on the other hand, may have felt reasonably secure with the support of Western countries who have veto power in the Security Council. It is, nevertheless, a prime target for UN economic sanctions, which would go beyond the existing arms sales embargo and OAU and Arab boycotts, and which might be imposed to make sanctions against Rhodesia more effective, and/or to force action by South Africa on Namibia and the elimination of apartheid. As noted in Chapter 5, South Africa is particularly vulnerable to an oil embargo. A report from the UN Special Committee on Apartheid published in 1978 asserted that ". . . without the continued supply of oil, the South African economy would rapidly grind to a halt".[6] That the South African government has not failed to grasp the vital significance of oil is illustrated by its promulgation of stringent regulations concerning secrecy in all matters concerning its production and marketing; by designating oil as a strategic commodity which must be made available for government purchase; and by other measures requiring maintenance of reserves and forbidding restrictions on sales.[7] The recent change of government in Iran which produced a new policy banning oil supplies to South Africa is a matter of serious concern to the Republic; as noted in Chapter 3, Iran has been its major source of oil since the OAPEC countries imposed an embargo in 1973.

Typical advance action by potential targets to reduce the effect of embargoes on imports includes stockpiling, the development of alternative sources of supply, the stimulation and diversification of domestic production, control of scarce and strategic resources and the development of industrial substitutes. Conservation of physical resources can be matched by conservation of gold and foreign exchange; additional means of transportation can be acquired, particularly merchant vessels and tankers, and new transport routes developed. In the wider sphere of inter-state economic relations new links can be forged, new trade agreements signed, and new markets opened up. A policy of cultivating neighbours and friends may well pay dividends during a sanctioning episode and reduce its impact. Some of these measures are worth considering in more detail.

Stockpiling

Where an essential raw material or commodity is obtainable only from an external source, and perishability (at least over a reasonable period) is not a serious problem, the obvious precautionary measure to meet a possible stoppage of supply is to accumulate stocks within the country. Storage space may be inadequate initially, in which case additional containers and stores may have to be built. Investment in additional stocks of goods and in storage facilities may be partially or wholly financed by the government.

In 1968 the South African government asked importers of chemicals and rubber to accumulate a stockpile equal to six months' normal supply, and as early as 1965 the major oil companies were instructed to make similar provisions. Subsequently, three extensive tank 'farms' were built by the government – at Durban, Port Elizabeth, and Cape Town – and disused mines are used as storage tanks for oil. The size of these reserves is a closely guarded secret. In Rhodesia, there was limited capacity for storage of refined products, but stocks built up by the oil companies before UDI allowed about four weeks to devise procedures for importing oil before the first British government sanctions order took effect on 16 December 1965.[8]

Since the 1973 Arab oil embargo, reserve stocks of oil have been built up by all western nations, and are required of members of the International Energy Agency.

Development of alternative external sources of supply

As a supplement or alternative to stockpiling, the government and business sectors of a country threatened with sanctions may seek to develop new sources of supply for essential imports. Over-dependence on any one source is undesirable; a multiplicity of sources will make an embargo on exports to the target more difficult to put into effect. It will be particularly useful if connections can be built up, in advance of sanctions, with countries outside the prospective sanctioning group, or with those inside it who are least enthusiastic about collective action. South Africa developed close trading links with France and Japan; military equipment was obtained from France despite the Security Council resolution recommending an arms embargo, and in return France became an important purchaser of South African uranium.

Trade agreements which confer benefits on both parties may be concluded, ensuring the continuation of supplies to the target. If the latter has worthwhile concessions to offer, its bargaining position will be strengthened. It is possible that goods supplied in terms of such agreements will not be affected by sanctions; they may be exempted as "contracts in process of execution", as occurred in the Italian, and initially, in the Rhodesian cases. These new trade alignments may be to the advantage of third countries which formerly had little access to the markets of the target because of the strength of competition, established habits of importing, and other factors such as preferential tariffs.

Stimulation and diversification of production

While it is in the material interest of any economy, however well developed, to pursue goals of increased production and higher living standards, a country finding itself threatened by economic penalties for pursuing a policy which it is determined not to abandon may give priority to achieving a greater degree of self-sufficiency, and be prepared to forgo some of the benefits of exchange.

Imports can be reduced by official controls, particularly over non-essential items. As all imports have to be paid for ultimately by gold or by foreign currency drawn from reserves or earned by exports, and as a sanctions policy is likely to involve a boycott of at least some exports from the target, there will be an added incentive to reduce the quantity of imports by volume and value in order to conserve foreign exchange.

Where there is already a sound industrial base, and a reasonably high level of domestic saving, it will be possible for government to encourage the expansion of secondary industry by giving financial assistance to approved projects, by offering tax incentives to manufacturers, and by participating in the establishment of new industries. It may also be possible to develop indigenous sources of supply of essential raw materials. Dependence on imported oil encouraged the South African government to finance a costly, though unsuccessful, exploration programme both on land and offshore. It has also invested heavily in expanding the domestic production of oil from coal. SASOL I, an oil from coal plant, produces about 4,500 barrels per day, which is only one per cent of current consumption, but in 1980–81 SASOL II will come into production and this will bring the percentage of domestically produced oil up to at least 12 per cent and possibly higher. According to a UN Report, cost estimates more than doubled from R1.0 million to R2.5 million between 1974 and 1977[9] and a recent announcement by the South African government of a rise in the price of petrol was linked to the projected doubling of the capacity of SASOL II, to cost R3.3 million.[10]

In order to reduce dependence on foreign trade, a government which fears sanctions may deliberately encourage the research and development of satisfactory substitutes. In modern industrial states there is considerable scope for such projects, particularly through the expansion of the petro-chemical industry. In the agricultural sphere new crops can be tried out, and food production increased by assistance to farmers.

DEFENCE OF THE ECONOMY UNDER SANCTIONS

If economic sanctions are imposed it will be to the advantage of all sections of the community to minimize the effect on their economic life. This is a defensive reaction which does not preclude prior and continuing political opposition to the policy which led to sanctions in the first place. In other words, a government which decides to resist sanctions can probably rely on economic co-operation at all levels. It is a weakness of economic sanctions that they automatically produce defensive measures which detract from their efficacy and may even render them counter-productive in some areas.

In making a political decision to resist sanctions, the government of the target will be influenced by many factors, in which prestige and the need to save face may be important. It will also be necessary to estimate in economic terms the extent to which sanctions can be endured and evaded. There may have been advance notice, giving time for anticipatory action of the kind already described, but in any case the defence of the economy under conditions of siege or partial siege will call for new strategies.

Adaptive measures can be considered under two headings: defensive measures to increase self-sufficiency and reduce dependence on the outside world, and the development of new links with states that are not participating fully in sanctions. It may also be useful to take counter-measures designed to damage sanctionists and induce them to abandon their coercive effort. All three policies are likely to be followed. The costs of resistance, to the extent that it can be estimated, may be acceptable as an additional cost of the policy which the target refuses to alter or modify: in this case, the penalty of economic damage becomes a type of fine which the target is prepared to pay.

If embargoes on exports to the targets are effective, their immediate effect will be to deprive normal users of access to these goods. In some cases, such as raw materials which are not available locally, stockpiling and rationing may be instituted and efforts made to obtain supplies elsewhere. In other cases, such as machinery and parts, existing stocks can be made to last longer by 'stretching' and equipment can be cannibalized. Extra effort can be demanded from men and machines to meet the crisis; retirement and replacement can be postponed. Ironically, the benefits of modernization of plant may accrue to industry at the end of the crisis.

The ingenuity of advanced industrial economies in managing without 'essential' raw materials and minerals has been noteworthy in both world wars of this century, while the mobilization of national effort in the Soviet Union since 1917, and Germany's deliberately sought policy of autarky in the 1930s are convincing examples of the ability of powerful states to go it alone and to exert counter-pressure. Moreover, the techniques of managing economies are well developed even in states which are not organized on a central plan system, and no government is now unaware of the means by which controls can be exercised over the functioning of the economic system, especially on a beggar-my-neighbour basis. Economic nationalism could be an unwelcome product of economic sanctions.

There is no doubt that deprivation can act as a powerful stimulus to the growth of industry. Examples can be given from South Africa, Australia, and Rhodesia during the Second World War. Furthermore, if a state is committed to policies of self-sufficiency, an embargo policy imposed by other nations can be helpful. Susan Strange, writing about the Western strategic embargoes on trade with Communist countries, commented that these policies "militated against the self-interest of the Western alliance by forcing the Soviet bloc into even greater self-sufficiency in the means of making modern war than it would otherwise have attained".[11] South Africa has reacted similarly.

In some instances embargoes on exports to the target state may act as a stimulant to domestic production. The elimination of foreign competition will provide a form of protection to local producers. Investment in production for the enlarged home market will become more profitable, and for consumers there will be the added spur of patriotic feeling, encouraging them to buy home-produced goods. A full-scale programme of economic sanctions can have similar effects: by blocking normal channels of supply it may provide a forcing ground for industrial expansion – and for increased agricultural production in the target. It was noted in Chapter 5 that all these features were characteristic of the response of Rhodesian domestic industry and Rhodesian consumers under United Nations sanctions. Development and diversification in manufacturing, in agriculture and in the processing of agricultural products helped to offset the deterioration in certain sectors of the economy, particularly in the tobacco industry.

Where exports from the target are banned as imports into sanctionist states, even if exports to the target are not subject to embargo, the resulting limitation of foreign exchange earnings will make import control advisable. Luxury and non-essential imports may be prohibited, or drastically restricted, and other imports controlled by a licence-quota system. Quotas may be allocated to imports on a *pro rata* basis, as a percentage of their imports in a normal, pre-crisis year. If necessary consumer goods can be rationed, and consumption can also be held in check by taxation and exhortations to save, backed by the issue of savings bonds. Scarce materials can be allocated to industry on a quota basis; labour may be directed into important jobs, and if sanctions causes unemployment problems, government schemes for maintaining employment may be instituted. Special compensatory action may be taken to assist groups particularly hard hit by sanctions; alternatively the dominant political group may shift some of the impact of sanctions to less privileged groups. For instance, in Rhodesia, it was possible for white employment levels to be protected at the expense of African workers. Monetary and fiscal policy can also be adjusted to counter strains on the economy over a period of time. All these measures, which correspond broadly to those which are usually imposed by a government in time of war, can be justified in terms of the crisis, particularly if there is a national will to resist sanctions.

Writing on the Italian response to sanctions, M. J. Bonn noted that "stocks on hand, the practice of economies, the development of substitutes, and the purchase of goods with gold, foreign securities, emigrants' remittances and tourists' disbursement kept the country going without too severe a strain."[12] The government of Rhodesia used many of the same methods to meet the strains imposed on the economy by sanctions. Shortages of consumer goods developed, some of a temporary nature, but only petrol was formally rationed.

RELIANCE ON NON-SANCTIONISTS

The implications of partial participation for effective programmes of economic denial were discussed at some length in the previous chapter. It will be particularly convenient for the target of sanctions if non-participants are neighbours, or if they are powerful enough to give substantial aid. Generalizations are impossible for circumstances will vary from case to case, but the support of non-sanctionists will always be valuable, and may be crucial for surviving economic sanctions. Such support has been sought and received by countries subjected to regional economic pressure as well as by Italy under League sanctions and Rhodesia under United Nations sanctions. Yugoslavia, Albania, China, and Cuba all re-oriented their trade as a result of regional deprivation, and although they may have been 'better off' with their former relationships and patterns of trading, their survival, through their own efforts and those of their friends undermined the sanctions effort. The existence of non-sanctionists also facilitates sanctions evasion which is discussed in the next section.

EVASION OF SANCTIONS

It is hardly necessary to stress the endless possibilities for evading sanctions by 'illegal' means. Smuggling becomes highly profitable for middlemen who can charge an inflated commission and in the target state, it will have official blessing if it succeeds in systematically disposing of exports or obtaining imports through clandestine channels. Complicated systems of staged delivery can be worked out, and this process will be made easier if friendly countries allow themselves to be used as intermediate supply points. Where certificates of origin are called for, they can be falsified. Equally complicated, but no less efficient financial arrangements can be devised to overcome difficulties of payment.

Commercial interests which have no concern with the objectives of sanctions will be deterred from the chance to make additional profits or from the prospect of sustaining severe loss only if heavy penalties are likely to be incurred and enforced. This presupposes an efficient system of inspection and control within the borders of sanctionist states which probably does not exist. One of the major problems in detecting evasion of sanctions by Rhodesia has been the use of bills of lading and Chamber of Commerce certificates emanating from South Africa; these have often to be accepted as sufficient proof of origin although the UN Sanctions Committee has asked member governments to seek additional documentation wherever possible. This is both complicated and time-consuming;

for instance, the UK government which, in spite of its awareness that oil was reaching Rhodesia in quantities adequate for the survival of the economy, has been assiduous in reporting suspicions of sanctions evasion to the UN, noted that a network of companies in South Africa, Switzerland and other European countries were involved in importing minerals of Rhodesian origin.[13] A variety of agents, buyers, ships and planes under charter, constitute a labyrinth which may be relatively impenetrable.

Financial transactions, like commercial transactions can be passed through a number of intermediaries ("laundered" in Watergate parlance) so that the original sources and the ultimate destination are disguised. The raising of capital for the expansion of the Rhodesian Iron and Steel Corporation (RISCO) plant at QueQue is a case in point; details which came to light after investigation show the interposition of a South African company (the South African Steel Corporation (Pty) Ltd.) between loans arranged by Swiss interests and ultimate recipients.[14]

The cases which the Security Council Sanctions Committee has investigated – in all about 350 – illustrate graphically the points made above, and the Bingham and Commonwealth Secretariat reports on oil sanctions to which reference has been made in earlier chapters show only too clearly how a neighbouring state can render export embargoes quite useless. The case of oil deserves special attention because of the strategic nature of oil as a commodity and because of the full account which is now available of how sanctions were evaded.

Oil for Rhodesia

Given the dependence of Rhodesia on imported petroleum, there was no doubt of the significance of the embargo imposed by Britain and Commonwealth countries in 1965 and by the Security Council in 1966. Equally, for the Rhodesian government, evasion of this sanction was crucial for its survival from the outset. In earlier chapters reference has been made to the system of 'swap' arrangements using South African subsidiaries of major oil companies to circumvent the oil embargo. Although the details of these arrangements have only been fully revealed in recent years, it has been obvious since UDI that oil supplies to Rhodesia were at no time subject to serious disruption; it was also clear that the only effective means of checking this flow would be to cut oil supplies to South Africa. This was a step Britain and other western powers were not prepared to take. External pressure on South African subsidiaries of major oil companies was of no avail, since under South African law these subsidiaries must sell oil to all customers at the current price and may not set conditions for sale. A South African firm, Freight Services Ltd., acted as intermediary between the subsidiaries and GENTA, the Rhodesian government agency set up in January 1966 to handle oil imports.

In 1964 Rhodesian consumption of oil products was 9,000 barrels per day (b/d); Bailey and Rivers estimate that at the time of their report the comparable figure was 16,000 b/d.[15] Once the oil pipeline from Beira to the Ferruka refinery at Umtali was closed, it became necessary for Rhodesia to import refined oil products, rather than crude oil (i.e. petrol, aviation and diesel fuel and non-fuel products such as lubricants). Until the border closure in 1976, some refined oil products could reach Rhodesia from the refinery at Maputo (formerly Lourenço Marques), but the bulk of imports emanated from foreign-owned refineries in the Republic of South Africa, particularly Durban refineries which were the nearest to Mozambique. The route used was to ship oil to Maputo and Beira from South Africa (and from the Persian Gulf) and thence transport it by rail to Rhodesia. By the time this route was closed in 1976, a new South African-Rhodesian rail link had been completed and this provided an alternative route, more direct than using the older South African-Rhodesian rail link through Botswana. By keeping the oil in bond between South Africa and Rhodesia, customs duties were not involved and South Africa and Mozambique trade statistics did not reflect these transactions.

The United Church of Christ in the US published a report in 1976 setting out the kind of "paper-chase" which South Africa and Rhodesia devised to conceal the means by which oil was being channelled to Rhodesia, in this case using Mobil subsidiaries.[16] Bailey and Rivers point out that all five major oil companies – Mobil, Caltex (US), Shell (Dutch-British), BP (British), Total (French) – were probably involved in similar schemes.[17] The church group's report cites secret documents which note the importance of laying false trails and complicating processes of purchase and sale through a sequence of customers in order to "discourage investigation" and conceal the contravention of US and other national sanctions regulations by South African subsidiaries of companies registered in those countries.[18]

It transpired that the process of investigating the authenticity of documents obtained by such bodies as the United Church of Christ, as well as of laying bare the full ramifications of oil company subsidiaries' complicity in supplying oil to Rhodesia was blocked in South Africa by the Official Secrets Act which made any such investigation illegal for South African nationals, or for nationals of other countries (e.g. officials of Mobil or Caltex from the US head offices of these companies).

Publication in Britain of the Report of the Haslemere Group and the Anti-Apartheid movement in March 1977 raised the question whether Shell and BP were also involved in supplying Rhodesia with oil. As BP is 51 per cent British government-owned, with two government appointed directors, this was a serious matter. Further publicity and concern followed disclosure in the *Sunday Times* of 10 April 1977 that Lonrho, a mining conglomerate, would sue the oil majors for breaking their 1962 agreement to use the Beira-Umtali pipeline (62 per cent Lonrho-owned) as the sole means of supplying oil to Rhodesia, and that the United African Council of Zimbabwe had requested further hearings of the US Senate on the question, claiming new information. Bailey and Rivers point out that this information was largely supplied by Lonrho.[19] This led to the establishment of an official inquiry in Britain with the objects of establishing "the facts concerning operations whereby suppliers of petroleum and petroleum products have reached Rhodesia since December 1965 . . . and the extent, if any, to which persons and companies within the scope of the sanctions order (1968) have played any part in such operations".[20] Mr. Thomas H. Bingham, Q. C., and Mr. S. M. Gray were subsequently appointed to carry out this inquiry, which had a wider scope than the US Treasury inquiry into the allegations against Mobil of a year earlier which was concerned with the possible violation of US law.

These developments led to renewed demands at the Security Council and at the Commonwealth Heads of Government meeting in June 1977 for a tightening up of sanctions and the report *Oil Sanctions against Rhodesia*[21] was the outcome of further study by the Commonwealth Committee on Southern Africa undertaken at the specific request of the Commonwealth summit.

The Bingham Report, published in 1978, noted "important obstacles" to obtaining necessary information: (a) South African legislation which makes it a criminal offence to ". . . communicate

information concerning oil stocks and supplies . . ." and (b) the
inability or unwillingness of parent companies of major foreign oil
companies "to give detailed assistance on the facts"; (c) the non-
cooperation of the governments of Zambia, Mozambique and
South Africa; (d) the lapse of time (12 years) since sanctions were
imposed which meant loss of records and loss of memory.[22]

Nevertheless, the Report is able to confirm that from 1968 to the
end of 1971, Total South Africa, a subsidiary of the French group
Compagnie Francaises des Petroles, supplied oil to Freight Services
(which in turn sold it to the Rhodesian agency GENTA) in
exchange for a similar amount supplied to it in South Africa by the
consolidated marketing group of Shell and BP and that the British
government were aware of the 'swap' arrangement almost from
the outset.[23] After 1971 this arrangement ceased and Shell
Mozambique, (registered in Britain) became part of the chain of
supply until the closure of the Rhodesia-Mozambique border in
March 1976. Thereafter South African companies (SASOL or
SASRAF) took on the responsibility for supplying Freight Services
and Shell and BP's South African subsidiaries who had dissolved
their Consolidated Agreements in September 1975, were probably
not involved in the trade.[24] Of course, Shell and BP subsidiaries in
Rhodesia had been subject to Rhodesian government orders since
UDI and would have been liable to criminal penalties for non-
compliance; in the same way, South African subsidiaries were
subject to the laws of the Republic. The problems of overlapping
jurisdiction were often acute.

The oil companies were obviously caught in not one but two
cross-pressure situations. On the one hand, British and South
African government policies were diametrically opposed on the
question of sanctions against Rhodesia; on the other, the British
government while sponsoring sanctions and introducing orders to
implement them did not want any economic confrontation with
South Africa. Technicalities provided an escape route for the
government; indirect supply could be tolerated, while direct supply
was avoided.

The Bingham Report's conclusion that failures by Shell and BP
to disclose the mechanisms in place between 1971 and 1976 put
the British government in the unfortunate position of giving
"assurances which they would not have done with full knowledge of
the facts" is incontrovertible. To the analyst the difference between
the technically legal position of not being directly part of the chain

of supply of oil to Rhodesia and the technically illegal position of being directly involved may seem a matter of degree rather than of substance; the more important point is that the flow of oil to Rhodesia could only have been checked by confronting or blockading South Africa – a step which no major external power, including the British government, was prepared to take. In practical terms the oil sanction imposed by the UN against Rhodesia was no more effective than the League's failure to impose a similar penalty on Italy in 1936.

COUNTER-SANCTIONS

As an additional means of maintaining its position, the government of a country subjected to sanctions may decide to take positive retaliatory action in the form of counter-sanctions. Their effect will vary according to the degree of dependence of sanctionist states on their economic relations with the target; in some cases, states may be even more vulnerable to counter-sanctions than the target is to sanctions.

When Lesotho and Botswana became independent in 1966, the governments of both countries publicly qualified their ability and willingness to take part in any international sanctioning programme in Southern Africa on the grounds of their vulnerability to counter-sanctions, and this was accepted by the UN. But such vulnerability is not restricted to small, poor and less-developed countries. It is inevitable that where two countries are mutually linked by a network of economic relationships they are, in effect, hostages of each other; the loss for both as a result of sanctions will be considerable. There may be a special vulnerability to counter-sanctions and self-sufficiency may also have to be cultivated by sanctionists. South Africa's importance to the west as a major exporter of gold and other vital raw materials for which the alternative source of supply is the Soviet Union, makes counter-sanctions by the Republic a contingency to be reckoned with, whether as a response to direct sanctions or to pressure by UN members to enforce compliance with sanctions against Rhodesia. The Prime Minister of South Africa warned Shell and BP in 1967 that a deterioration in relations would follow interference with the activities of their South African subsidiaries; the companies and the British government feared sequestration of assets.

Financial counter-sanctions must also be considered, particularly debt repudiation which is a simple means of striking back and, at the same time, ridding oneself of onerous obligations. Italy exacted a belated penalty from the countries which imposed sanctions upon her by meeting financial obligations to post-sanctions creditors before discharging pre-sanctions debts. Soon after UDI Rhodesia blocked payments to residents of Britain, Zambia and the US and repudiated interest payable on debts to Britain and for which the British government was the guarantor including a World Bank loan. Britain as the responsible power had to meet these charges. Strack notes that financial counter-sanctions relieved Rhodesia of "making capital repayments and interest payments on an obligation of about £160 million".[25]

Expropriation of property is another familiar weapon. The Cuban government nationalized sugar plantations and processing plants, oil refineries, and electric and telephone companies belonging to United States interest as a declared reprisal for the cut in the sugar quota; this led to a total embargo on trade with Cuba being imposed by the United States. Counter-embargoes on food or other commodities were discussed in the US during and following the Arab oil embargo; a Congressional Report concluded that "on the basis of the data available, leverage available to the Arabs through their oil boycott far exceeds any leverage that might be available to the United States through a food embargo since the Arabs can meet their relatively small food import needs from other sources in the world market while the United States cannot meet its relatively large petroleum import needs from other sources".[26] But if the US were to cut all food exports, the effects on the rest of the world could be considerable.

PUBLIC OPINION AND MORALE

The assumption that collective measures taken under international auspices will encourage internal opposition to the government of the target and bring about a change in policy is based on the belief that the burden of economic hardship imposed by sanctions will become intolerable. It may also be hoped that popular identification with the offending policy will weaken because it has been internationally condemned. But if a core value, such as white supremacy, is at stake, this hope may prove ill-founded. And in the face of an external threat it is by no means axiomatic that internal divisions will increase; instead a consolidation of public feeling may occur, and there may be a heightened sense of solidarity and national purpose. Moreover, in seeking to induce political change by economic sanctions, it will also be necessary to consider the political significance of different sections of the population and the ability of the electorate to make informed and accurate judgments of the economic and political situation. To some extent people will be guided by their leaders and if they retain confidence in them may be persuaded that a change in policy, in the face of external pressure, is not in their best interests or those of the country as a whole.[27]

The point is also worth making that sanctions can provide leaders with a useful explanation for any economic difficulties or setbacks which may be encountered in the target state, whether or not these have any connection with international enforcement measures. It is often difficult to distinguish between or to identify causes of economic difficulty, but always convenient to blame them on outside agencies. Both in Cuba and in Rhodesia sanctions have been so blamed.

A government determined to resist sanctions will make every effort to rally public opinion behind its policy of non-compliance. Public morale will be crucial and can be bolstered by skilful propaganda. A willingness to make sacrifices and adapt to short-ages, commonly associated with a war effort, is likely to emerge among citizens of the target state, and will be sedulously fostered by a sophisticated government. Instead of economic deprivation serving to undermine the government in the target state, it may have a politically integrative effect and strengthen its position. A siege psychosis, once engendered, can be a powerful factor in sustaining the will to resist, and it will also enable the government to take unpopular steps such as rationing consumer goods or increasing taxes. There is a danger too, that in evoking this defiant reaction, there may be less readiness to compromise than before sanctions were imposed, so that a peaceful solution of the crisis becomes more and not less difficult to achieve. This may affect both sanctionist and sanctioned. The former, having committed themselves to a policy of coercion, may demand unrealistic concessions to justify the termination of sanctions, while compromise by the government of the target state may appear as a betrayal of national values to its citizens. If the issues appear clear cut and national feeling has been roused in support of resistance to sanctions, capitulation would look like defeat, and it will be more difficult for the government of the country to adopt a more conciliatory attitude without loss of face. It may well fear that public reaction will lead to its dismissal by the electorate, and its replacement by a more intransigent group of leaders.

One of the most interesting features of the League sanctions experiment was the extent to which the Italian people rallied behind Mussolini. Baer notes that "what was meant to be only instrumental economic pressure to elicit internal protest was transformed by the Italian government into a cause for rapid intensification of integral economic and political national-ism. . . . sanctions made the Ethiopian war popular".[28]

In post-war programmes of economic denial, the typical reaction has been defiance. It is true that the Arab oil embargo 'worked' against Western Europe and Japan but it required no more than a foreign policy shift which would no doubt be supported by most citizens who saw a vital commodity threatened. But the US reaction was sharper and it seems unlikely that a US government would submit meekly to external pressure over an extended period. And although the US has put pressure on Israel to make peace with Egypt, it has not abandoned Israel as an ally. China, Yugoslavia, and Albania and Cuba failed to succumb to economic pressure and in South Africa there has also been defiance. Although it has been faced with the disapproval of the whole world, expressed repeatedly and in the strongest terms, the South African government has not only maintained and even intensified its policies of racial discrimi-nation, but has received strong support from the white electorate. Concern in the Republic about possible United Nations action is obvious but the typical white South African attitude is one of hostility to 'world opinion' which is presented by government-controlled media as uninformed and misguided as to the true position in the country, and inspired by world communism.

A similar reaction was evident in Rhodesia. Although there were elements in the white electorate who did not support the idea of UDI, there was a general willingness to try to make it work afterwards, and the rank and file of Rhodesian Front supporters remained loyal to the Smith regime which was the effective government of the country. Guerrilla incursions from across the Rhodesian border initially stiffened the resolve to preserve white supremacy. Over a longer period, however, it proved impossible for the Rhodesian government to maintain a high level of morale. The tenacity of purpose of African states in seeking to eliminate white rule in Southern Africa; the increasing isolation of Rhodesia as Angola and Mozambique joined the ranks of opposition and gave assistance to guerrilla forces; the diminishing level of political and military support from South Africa and the increasing level of guerrilla activity inside Rhodesia combined to outweigh the earlier confidence that economic sanctions were being overcome and would eventually be removed or "wither away".

The major problem for Rhodesia and for South Africa in sustaining high morale over a long period is obviously the fact that the majority of the population in both countries is opposed to white minority rule and if South African and Rhodesian blacks openly ally themselves with outside forces or succeed in becoming organized as effective political or military agents of change, the fortress can crumble from within. Nor is it easy in the late 20th century to maintain the legitimacy of positions based on white supremacy.

EXTERNAL PROPAGANDA

The government of the target state will not only take such counter-measures as it deems advisable; as a corollary to conducting a vigorous propaganda campaign at home in order to sustain public support, it will also be likely to employ all available means of persuading public opinion in the rest of the world that it has right on its side and is a victim of unjust action. It may threaten further counter-measures, and it will attempt to win sympathy for its cause, in the interest of weakening the sanctions front.

In a propaganda campaign of this type, diplomatic activity can be supplemented by government information services; by fostering the formation and activities of groups and societies friendly to the cause; and by using the services of advertising agencies and employing all available media of communication. Such propaganda will be intensified if the government of the target is under the impression that a negotiated settlement not involving the abandonment of its policy is possible.

Mussolini's government was extremely active on the diplomatic front and attempted to rally the support of Italian communities resident in other parts of the world, particularly in the United States and Latin America. At an early meeting of the League Co-ordinating Committee, the Argentine delegate pointed out that the population of his country included about a million Italians, and for this reason a strict application of Article 16 to Italy would be very controversial.

The South African government, for its part, has conducted an elaborate propaganda campaign for many years in which the official activities of the State Information Office have been supplemented by the work of private bodies such as the South African Foundation.[29] In the case of Rhodesia, early propaganda emphasized the fact that Rhodesian pilots (including Prime Minister Ian Smith) fought in the Battle of Britain in 1940, and that white Rhodesians were 'kith and kin' of British people. The ability of the Rhodesian government to maintain law and order was contrasted with the instability of regimes in independent Africa; the most favourable light was shed on conditions in the country, while determination to maintain independence in face of United Nations condemnation was repeatedly stressed. The Communist conspiracy was cited regularly as responsible for anti-Rhodesian action (a theme which is, of course, also pursued in South Africa) and the presence of Cuban forces in Angola and later in Ethiopia gave some credence to this line of argument, particularly to elements of western opinion which fear the spread of communism and wish to contain it. Rhodesia maintained information offices in Australia and the US (until the governments of these countries closed them in 1974 and 1977 respectively) and Friends of Rhodesia societies were formed in many overseas countries to undertake unofficial lobbying and public relations work.

Exclusion from international organizations effectively deprives governments of an important forum in which to present their case and answer the charges made by those who condemn them. This has been the fate of both Rhodesia and South Africa, and pressure has been exerted by Arab countries to exclude Israel from the UN and other bodies. The implications of this international isolation are discussed further in Chapter 8.

8 Conclusion

In Chapter One, the scope of the inquiry was defined as encompassing recent experience with collective recourse to economic coercion for political ends, particularly by bodies claiming some authority to impose sanctions as penalities for non-compliance with international standards. The effectiveness and the costs of such programmes, as well as their justification were stated as major subjects for investigation. In attempting to draw the threads together in this final chapter, the first point must be that the cases examined offer little evidence that economic sanctions provide reliable means of inducing states to adhere to internationally acceptable codes of conduct.

The purpose of a sanction is to control behaviour and it must rely for its effectiveness on a number of factors. Among these, its deprivational impact may be of less consequence than the status of the norm or rule it seeks to uphold and the status of the political system of which it is a part. This status is a function of legality and of legitimacy: in a system which commands respect and which is seen by citizens as supporting those standards and institutions which they value in their society, political authorities will have legitimized as well as legal standing. Norms are likely to be observed in such a framework, particularly if they reflect broadly accepted values.[1] Where legitimacy is in question, a firm, sustained level of enforcement within a state may succeed in maintaining conformity with law. In 'police states' fear of sanctions will play a greater role, although violence and civil strife in many parts of the world bear testimony to the difficulty of maintaining law and order where challenges to legitimacy have strong roots. And even in more democratic societies law is not always enforceable; powerful corporations, trade unions and other organized groups are not easily controlled.

International organizations lack some of the advantages of national governments and share their weaknesses. In exercising authority they do not enjoy assured legal or legitimized status and are unlikely to generate strong feelings of fear or respect. Although some leadership may be given by their executive heads – Dag Hammarsjold being the outstanding example – for the most part they are dependent on their members for the will and resources to act. These members are nation-states whose governments give precedence to the promotion and defence of what are seen as national interests and do not generally accept that policy on major issues can be dictated to them by international bodies. The state claims the loyalty and obedience of its citizens, standing between them and international organizations and is rarely bypassed by direct channels of communication.[2]

There is the further problem that norms of required behaviour are ill-defined and uncertain at the international level. Pledges in the UN Charter to promote economic development and human rights obviously permit progress to vary considerably in pace and even to come to a halt, while more specific rules are qualified in the interests of protecting state sovereignty. Thus the Charter's ban on the use of armed force does not apply if self-defence is deemed necessary. The history of the last thirty-five years is full of arguments about the priorities which should be given to peace, self-determination, majority rule, economic justice and other goals, and about the legality of the use of threats, force and other means of pressure to achieve them. Even where an inter-governmental consensus on culpability might be assumed to exist, it is not invariably expressed publicly and even more rarely leads to the imposition of collective penalties on the offender. Rhetorical and symbolic forms of censure are less costly than double-edged economic or military sanctions and may be preferred to them, although it should be noted that repeated collective condemnation at the United Nations, particularly when no improvement in the offending situation seems to follow, can set up pressures on members of the group to do something more. Western powers have experienced such pressures in respect of their position on race discrimination in Southern Africa. Indeed, it has been the achievement of African countries – and of the civil rights movement, particularly in the United States – to establish the general unacceptability of racial discrimination against blacks. When this norm of non-discrimination is linked to self-determination for people formerly under colonial rule, or for the abolition of apartheid and white minority rule, it gathers additional moral force and provides one of the few issues on which political consensus has been attainable at the United Nations. White regimes in Southern Africa have become increasingly isolated; they find it impossible to challenge the UN norms externally and progressively more difficult to deny their validity internally, particularly as the majority of their population – given a free choice – would support them.

Sanctions against Rhodesia and South Africa derive status and credibility from their relation to a universal norm; the United Nations as well as bodies with more limited membership such as the Commonwealth and the Organization of African Unity have condemned the policies and practices of both governments and imposed penalties. And even if the penalties, in themselves, have not proved decisive in bringing rapid change, their imposition must be seen as contributing to the erosion of white supremacy. Not all who supported economic sanctions against Rhodesia were also in favour of resort to force either by outside powers or by Rhodesian Africans, but the legitimacy of the Patriotic Front's position was enhanced because of UN sanctions and Rhodesia's failure, over a decade and a half, to comply fully with UN norms. The options for Rhodesia and South Africa have dwindled; they have been kept on the defensive in a progressively less defensible position; they have been excluded from normal participation in international conferences and institutions; the strains on their economies and social systems have been increased by external pressure. In the late 1970s, surrounded by black governments and under pressure not only from guerrilla forces in Namibia and Rhodesia but from Western powers who have major political and economic interests in the rest of Africa and who are anxious to stave off further Soviet intervention in the affairs of the continent, both Rhodesia and South Africa were ready to make concessions. A black-dominated parliament was elected in Rhodesia and a black Prime Minister took office; South Africa conceded the principle of independence for Namibia and sought to evade the dismantling of white supremacy in the Republic by creating 'independent' tribal homelands and by relaxing some of the regulations of petty apartheid.

The question arises whether consensus over Southern Africa is a unique case. Despite their condemnation of apartheid, which is a remarkably repugnant system in that a legal order entrenching racial discrimination simultaneously makes opposition to it a criminal offence, the Western powers have not shown themselves willing to impose general economic sanctions on South Africa. Other well-documented cases of gross abuse of human rights –

Uganda under Amin, Cambodia/Kampuchea, the Central African Empire – did not even produce universal, public censure.

At the regional level organizations and norms are not necessarily more fully legitimized. The issue would be clearer if sanctioning were restricted to the *external* behaviour of states – for instance, invasion of a neighbour's territory. But the use of force by states has become commonplace, and peacekeeping rather than peacemaking through the imposition of penalties has been the preferred international response. The group norms upheld by the United States and the Soviet Union in their respective spheres of influence have related to ideological orientation and internal policy: Cuba and Czechoslovakia were disciplined for deviation. In a just world, these targets of pressure might claim that their rights were trampled upon, and that sanctions should have been imposed against those 'sanctioning' them, but the realities of power have forced them to submit, or look for extra-regional help.

But if the moral force of sanctions often seems weaker at the regional than at the world level, comparable generalizations cannot be made about their economic and political impact. This study has shown the serious deficiencies in collective competence which international bodies exhibit. There is a low probability that sanctions will be invoked at all and a high probability that, if they are, there will be wide gaps in the sanctions net because of partial or non-participation and sanctions evasion. Loopholes in universal sanctions, as in the Rhodesian case, can be so serious that economic deprivation is minimized. Loopholes in regional sanctions may be wider still, so that Yugoslavia, Cuba and other targets were able to make up most of their lost trade elsewhere, – or they may be narrower. To close all gaps would require a comprehensive physical blockade, but where alternative sources of support and supply are not available the impact of economic measures will be greater, particularly if they have some 'bite' in relation to the economic circumstances of the target. The Arab oil embargo is the obvious example.

Willingness to resort to sanctions will reflect the value placed on upholding a group norm and the estimated cost of the measures to be used. Willingness to defy them will reflect the value placed on non-conformity and calculations of capacity to survive. Ironically, the pressure governments exert behind the scenes to impel others to adopt sanctions may be more persuasive than the sanctions themselves. Britain was perhaps under stronger pressure from the

Commonwealth to seek UN sanctions against Rhodesia than Rhodesia was, initially, to concede majority rule. Today, the Western powers are experiencing similar pressures over South Africa. But resort to economic sanctions is sure to be seriously questioned by governments when their own domestic problems loom large. Resource scarcity, unemployment, poor export performance and balance of payments difficulties will not readily and deliberately be compounded by assistance to causes which may be perceived as worthy, but which do not impinge closely upon national concerns or which might work against them. Governments making through the imposition of penalties has been the preferred may be forthcoming but action lags behind. In non-authorized situations the goals of economic coercion are likely to be closely related to national or group interest and measures will be directly aimed at the perceived vulnerabilities of the target. The OAPEC group were aware of the potential strength of the oil weapon when used against industrialized countries; it was seen as an effective weapon of economic warfare.

A further set of sanctions which can be used by international bodies deserves some attention in this chapter. The proliferation of international organizations since World War II, in response to the international character of many problems of security and welfare, has meant that much international business is now conducted within these frameworks. In turn, this has meant that the penalties of expulsion and exclusion from participation can be used as international political sanctions to reinforce economic sanctions or on their own. While international condemnation is reiterated at conferences and meetings and receives media publicity, the offending state is denied a voice and a vote.

In contrast to economic sanctions, these penalties can be readily implemented and are relatively cost-free, provided key states which contribute a major portion of the organization's resources are not the targets. Lesser powers, particularly those who are partially isolated within a region, are particularly vulnerable to multilateral political sanctions. The leaders of the sanctionists, or would-be sanctionists, can benefit from their strong stand in the eyes of their domestic supporters, and opposition groups cannot claim that they would do more, or better. And the censuring tactics may provide some useful 'cement' in holding a loose coalition together and producing consensus at international meetings. For the target state there are disadvantages. Its government has no opportunity to make its own case at international conferences and its critics go unchallenged. There is a loss of role and possibly a loss of access to services and resources. China, South Africa and Rhodesia have all suffered this treatment at the world level and exclusion from regional bodies has also been applied in some cases. Cuba's suspension from the OAS was noted in Chapter Three. At the UN level there is no alternative for the sanctioned state.

For Rhodesia, the witholding of international recognition has been most unwelcome. It has been deprived of the status it enjoyed before UDI when the Rhodesian Prime Minister attended Commonwealth Prime Ministers' meetings and Rhodesia had associate status in several UN agencies. China and South Africa did not forfeit recognition as sovereign states, but the Chinese government was denied representation at the United Nations for over twenty years, while South Africa has been excluded from the Commonwealth and from many UN agencies. Since 1974 it has also been unable to participate in General Assembly proceedings because of non-acceptance of its delegates' credentials. In recent years, Israel too has been challenged. Arab states denied its right to exist from the outset, but it became a member of the UN and its agencies and had normal diplomatic relationships outside the Arab world. But a majority in the General Assembly deemed Zionism to be a form of racism in 1974 and there have been efforts to exclude Israel from UNESCO.

Political isolation at the multilateral level, like the social sanctions on sporting links which Commonwealth members have applied to South Africa, represent a type of psychic coercion. To be condemned persistently by world opinion and excluded from international association is uncomfortable, particularly if friends become fewer and less openly friendly. Self-confidence may be undermined and the citizens of the target cannot always be 'protected' by censorship from learning of the hostility of the outside world. If their government's moral position is susceptible to challenge, opposition may grow. Rebels can identify with the external value system and in some circumstances they may hope for, or receive tangible as well as moral support: funds, arms, sanctuary and training facilities for guerrillas – as well as recognition at international conferences where government representatives are not welcome. Southern African and Palestinian liberation movements have been supported and welcomed at the United Nations and as their legitimacy is enhanced, so that of the governments they oppose is diminished. Given its low cost and high publicity value, the weapon of exclusion from international bodies is likely to commend itself for continued use by those who constitute the majority of their membership, although the standing of the organization itself will only be enhanced if its members take consistent stands on morally defensible positions.

As for economic coercion, it will doubtless continue to be an instrument of leverage used by governments in their own interests and sometimes in the interests of a wider group. In a framework of organization and in relation to a group norm, it can be dignified by the label of a sanction. Effectiveness must be judged on a case by case basis, and although authorized sanctions may have more symbolic value, the absence of authorization for collective measures does not necessarily rob them of efficacy. The crucial factors will be the nature of the objectives sought, their value to both coercor and coerced and the resources they are prepared to invest in them, as well as the target's ability to withstand pressure on its own, or with outside help. In a divided and economically interdependent world, such help is often forthcoming.

In contemporary international society the use of force does not generally commend itself as an appropriate form of coercion by international bodies. Economic sanctions have been viewed as alternatives, capable of producing an 'economic solution' instead of, and in preference to a 'military solution'. But except in the hypothetical cases of extreme vulnerability amounting to total economic dependence on the states imposing sanctions, or of universal economic ostracism, the coercive properties of economic sanctions are limited. Their impact can be reduced, overcome, or sustained, and the will to resist in the target may be strengthened. It is often argued that even if economic sanctions will not bring political compliance, they can usefully demonstrate international censure by damaging the economy of the offending state. But if these sanctions are no more than occasionally imposed and are not part of a recognized system of enforcement of legitimized norms by agencies which enjoy a respected status, this demonstration effect is open to serious question. Moreover, the deliberate impoverishment of a national economy, and possibly the economies of its neighbours, is out of line with the overriding and acknowledged need to promote economic development and raise living standards everywhere. The likelihood that the main burden of economic sanctions will be borne by the least privileged sections of the population in all affected states makes this argument even more cogent.

Acknowledgement of the limitations of economic sanctions does not mean that efforts should be relaxed which seek to curb gross violations of human rights wherever they occur. And in certain cases, international publicity and collective censure can be helpful. But the circumstances which contributed to the adoption of policies which the international community deems offensive also merit attention. White Rhodesians are not wholly to blame for the events which led up to UDI and its aftermath – some responsibility must be borne by Britain, just as the United States must take its share of responsibility for the chaos and misery in South-East Asia in the wake of the Vietnam war.

Coercion is an expensive means of social control, destructive of many of the values which it seeks to conserve. As statesmen grapple with a bewildering variety of economic problems which may defy solution but which urgently demand management, the emphasis in international political organizations should be placed on developing ways and means of lessening tension, keeping lines of communication open and avoiding conflict between their members. In the long run, this would be a more constructive approach to problem-solving than occasional resort to international 'enforcement' which suffers from all the limitations this study has revealed.

Notes

1. See Robert Engler, *The Politics of Oil* (Chicago, 1961); Peter Odell, *Oil and World Power* (1970); S. Chubin and Z. Sepehr, *The Foreign Relations of Iran* (Berkeley, 1974); US Senate, Committee on Foreign Relations, Subcommittee on Multinational Corporations, *Hearings on Multinational Corporations and United States Foreign Policy*, Parts I and II, 93rd Congress, 1st Session, 1973.
2. Cf. D. Mitrany, *The Problem of International Sanctions* (Oxford University Press, 1925): "the term . . . sanctions has now passed into general usage for describing collectively the various means prescribed or contemplated for enforcing international covenants", p. 1.
3. See D. W. Bowett, 'Economic Coercion and Reprisals by States', *The Virginia Journal of International Law*, Vol. 13, 1, 1972, pp. 1–12. See too R. Higgins, 'The Advisory Opinion on Namibia: which Resolutions are Binding under Article 25 of the Charter?' *International and Comparative Law Quarterly*, Vol. XXI (1972), pp. 270–86; O. Y. Asamoah, *The Legal Significance of the Declarations of the General Assembly* (1966).
4. Bowett points out that the Uniting for Peace Resolution and the subsequent work of the Collective Measures Committee tend to confirm the Assembly's power to 'authorize' economic sanctions. Loc. cit. n.23.
5. But GATT emphasises reciprocity, not enforcement, and sanctions are given a very limited place in the agreement. See K. Dam, *The GATT: Law and International Economic Organization* (Chicago, 1970), particularly pp. 352–64.
6. UN pressure on the World Bank to deny loan facilities to South Africa has been resisted. See S. A. Bleicher, 'UN v. IBRD: A Dilemma of Functionalism', *International Organization*, Vol. XXIV (1970), pp. 31–47.
7. The Treaty of Rome provides for the Commission to take a complaint that a member has failed to fulfil an obligation under the treaty to the European Court of Justice. Members may also take such complaints first to the Commission and then to the Court. The Court has authority to require member states to comply with its judgments. (Articles 169–171.)
8. See T. M. Franck & E. Weisband, *Word Politics* (1972), for an interesting comparison of the Brezhnev and Johnson doctrines.
9. Bowett, loc. cit., pp. 1–2.
10. General Assembly Resolution 2625(XV), 24 Oct. 1970. I. Brownlie notes that the Declaration's legal significance "lies in the fact that it provides evidence of the consensus among Member States of the UN on the meaning and elaboration of the principles of the Charter", *Basic Documents of International Law* (1968), p. 32.

11. Bowett, loc. cit., pp. 2–3.
12. Cf. General Assembly Resolution 1803 (XVII), 14 Dec. 1962, on Permanent Sovereignty over Natural Resources.
13. Thus Arab League penalties imposed on South Yemen in 1978 following the assassination of the North Yemeni President, for which South Yemen was held responsible, can be described as sanctions, whereas Arab measures against Israel must be justified as self-defence or reprisals. There is no regional code to which Israel can be expected to conform and the UN has not authorized any sanctions against Israel.
14. See below Chapter 2. See too R. B. Lillich, 'Economic Coercion and the International Legal Order', *International Affairs*, Vol. 51, 3 (1975), pp. 358–71.
15. Bowett, loc. cit., p. 9.

CHAPTER 2

1. See D. T. Jack, *Studies in Economic Warfare* (1940), pp. 1–42.
2. W. N. Medlicott, *The Economic Blockade*, i (1952), p. 9. The point is also made that new forms of neutral resistance were encountered.
3. See F. G. Tryon, 'How Germany met the Raw Materials Blockade 1914–1918' in Evans Clark (ed.), *Boycotts and Peace: A Report by the Committee on Economic Sanctions* (1932), pp. 338–49.
4. Medlicott, *Economic Blockade*, i, p. 3.
5. Germany's export trade was reduced "by 80 per cent of its normal value within a few months", Medlicott, *Economic Blockade*, ii (1959), p. 633.
6. Ibid., p. 659.
7. Ibid., p. 407–8, and J. B. Cohen, *Japan's Economy in War and Reconstruction* (1949).
8. Boycott, as in the case of the Arab boycott of Israel, may encompass a wide range of practices; in certain contexts it may be used in a limited sense to mean refusal to buy from unacceptable trading partners. An embargo in the narrow sense refers to a prohibition on sales and/or supplies.
9. See G. Adler-Karlsson, *Western Economic Warfare 1947–1967: A Case Study in Foreign Economic Policy* (Stockholm, 1968), pp. 51–2.
10. General Assembly Resolution 500(V), 18 May 1951. See below, Chapter 5.
11. In 1963 the 16th Battle Act *Report to Congress* noted that economic 'sanctions' had served only as a "marginal restraint" on Soviet aggressive capability during the Stalin and post-Stalin years. US Department of State, 1964, p. 8.
12. The Soviet Union subsequently refused to ratify a trade agreement with the US on the grounds that the Act constituted intervention in its domestic jurisdiction.
13. K. Grzybowski, 'East-West Trade Regulations in the United States: the 1974 US Trade Act, Title IV', *Journal of World Trade Law*, Vol. 11, No. 6 (Nov.–Dec. 1977), p. 14.
14. US Congress, Joint Economic Committee, *Report: Mainland China in the World Economy* (Washington, 1967), p. 8.
15. A. Eckstein (ed.), *China Trade Prospects and US Policy* (1971), p. xx.
16. T. A. Wolf, *US East-West Trade Policy* (1973), pp. xix–xx.

17. Resolution 357, 9 Mar. 1951. For a general account of the organization of the Arab boycott see *Textes Documentaires* (Damascus, Bureau des Documentations Syriennes et Arabes, Apr. 1956). See too D. S. Chill, *The Arab Boycott of Israel* (1976), written from a strong pro-Israeli standpoint.

18. See R. W. Macdonald, *The League of Arab States: a study of the dynamics of regional organization* (1965), particularly pp. 120–3.

19. Ibid.

20. See *New York Times*, 21 Nov. 1966.

21. *New York Times*, 13 Feb. 1975, 13 Mar. 1975. On 27 Nov. 1975 the *New York Times* published in full what was alleged to be the 1970 blacklist.

22. See Chill, op. cit., p. 47.

23. See the comments made in his personal capacity by D. A. Small, a State Department official, to the panel on 'Policy Conflicts in Foreign Trade and Investment', American Society of International Law, 72nd annual meeting, *Proceedings*, Apr. 1978, p. 83.

24. Public Law 95–52, 1977, Sec. 4A (a) (1).

25. But see F. Gervasi, *The Case for Israel* (1967), who suggests that the boycott "may have stimulated Israel's economic development by promoting greater self reliance", p. 134.

26. Cf. Sir T. Holland, *The Mineral Sanction as an Aid to International Security* (1935); R. Segal (ed.), *Sanctions against South Africa* 1964, pp. 135–152; J. E. Akins, 'The Oil Crisis: this time the Wolf is here', *Foreign Affairs*, Vol. 51, 3, 1973, pp. 463–90.

27. This is an average figure; oil producers such as Britain and Norway import under 50 per cent of their needs, while Italy imports about 85 per cent and France 66 per cent.

28. See US 94th Congress, 1st session. *Oil Fields as Military Objectives: a Feasibility Study*, a Report prepared for the House Committee on International Relations by the Congressional Research Service (Washington, 1975), for details of the dependence of the US and its major allies on imported oil and a discussion of the feasibility of using US military force to occupy foreign oil fields in the event of a future emergency.

29. Space does not permit a full listing of the flood of articles on the oil crisis, but the reader's attention is directed to J. J. Paust and A. P. Blaustein, *The Arab Oil Weapon* (1977), a valuable compendium of documentation and comment.

30. S. F. Singer, 'Limits to Arab Oil Power', *Foreign Policy*, No. 30, Spring 1978, p. 56.

31. See E. M. Shamsedin, *Arab Oil and the United States: an admixture of Politics and Economics*, University of South Carolina, Bureau of Business and Economic Research, No. 29, Apr. 1974; R. S. Pindyck, 'OPEC's Threat to the West', *Foreign Policy*, No. 30, Spring 1978, who notes that oil producers can dictate production levels but not the ultimate destination of their oil exports (pp. 45–6). See too *Oil Fields as Military Objectives*, Part I, note 2.

32. Kissinger's comments were made in an interview with *Business Week*, published on 13 Jan. 1975. See also a scenario for intervention in *Harper's*, Mar. 1975, pp. 45–62; R. W. Tucker, 'Oil; The Issue of American Intervention', *Commentary*, Jan. 1975, pp. 21–31.

33. US 93rd Congress, 1st session. *Data and Analysis Concerning the Possibility of a US Food Embargo as a Response to the Present Arab Oil Boycott*, prepared for the House

Committee on Foreign Affairs by the Congressional Research Service (Washington D.C., Nov. 1973).

34. See Paust and Blaustein op. cit., p. 191.
35. *Oil Fields as Military Objectives*, cited in n. 27 above.
36. Ibid., Part I.
37. Details in the *OECD Observer*, Nov. 1973, Jan.–Feb. 1975, pp. 20–5. France did not join the IEA but will be consulted.
38. Ian Smart has suggested that the oil weapon may be more useful for deterrence than compellence in the 1980s. See I. Smart in J. C. Hurewitz (ed.), *Oil, the Arab-Israeli Dispute and the Industrial World: Horizons of Crisis* (1976), p. 190. Soon after taking office in May 1979, the new Canadian government's declared intention to move the Canadian embassy in Israel from Tel Aviv to Jerusalem was 'postponed' after protests and scarcely veiled threats of economic retaliation by Arab leaders.
39. For a detailed argument claiming legality for the Arab case see I. F. Shihata, 'Destination Embargo of Arab Oil: its legality under international law', *American Journal of International Law*, Vol. 68, 4, 1974, pp. 591–627. This was a rejoinder to Paust and Blaustein's earlier attack on the legality of the embargo in the same journal, 'The Arab Oil Weapon: a threat to international peace', *AJIL* Vol. 68, 3, 1974, pp. 410–39. Both articles are reproduced in the Paust and Blaustein compendium, as well as a further rejoinder by the editors.

CHAPTER 3

1. For a full account of the measures against Yugoslavia see *White Book on Aggressive Activities by the Governments of the USSR . . . towards Yugoslavia* (Belgrade, Ministry of Foreign Affairs, 1951). Romania even cut rail and postal links with Yugoslavia in 1950.
2. See R. B. Farrell, *Yugoslavia and the Soviet Union 1948–1956: an Analysis with Documents* (Hamden, Conn., 1956); *UN Economic Survey of Europe in 1953* (Geneva, 1954), pp. 111–12.
3. F. E. Ian Hamilton, *Yugoslavia: Patterns of Economic Activity* (1968), p. 312; See too D. I. Rusinow, 'Yugoslav Development between East and West', *Journal of International Affairs*, Vol. 19, 2, 1965, pp. 181–93.
4. See Stefan C. Stolte, 'Albania under Economic Pressure from Moscow', *Bulletin* (Munich), Vol. 9, 3, 1962, pp. 25–34. Political aspects of the Soviet-Albanian rupture are described by M. Kaser, *Comecon: Integration Problems of the Planned Economies*, 2nd edition (1967), pp. 96–100.
5. See Anna P. Schreiber, 'Economic Coercion as an Instrument of Foreign Policy: US Economic Measures against Cuba and the Dominican Republic', *World Politics*, Vol. 25, Apr. 1973, particularly pp. 405–13; G. Connell-Smith, *The Inter-American System* (1966), pp. 246–50.
6. UN *Yearbook of International Trade Statistics, 1963* (New York, 1965), pp. 210–11.
7. Schreiber, 'Economic Coercion . . .', p. 409.
8. See R. St. J. Macdonald, 'The Organization of American States in Action', 15, *University of Toronto Law Journal* (1964), pp. 325–429; Jerome Slater, *Intervention*

and Negotiation: the United States and the Dominican Republic (1970), p. 8.

9. See J. Slater, 'The Limits of Legitimization in International Organization: the Organization of American States and the Dominican Crisis', *International Organization*, Vol. 23, 1, 1969, pp. 48–72.

10. Connell-Smith, op. cit., pp. 248–9.

11. US Department of State, *American Foreign Policy: Current Documents 1964* (Washington, 1967), pp. 323, 324.

12. US Department of State, Bureau of Intelligence and Research 1971, p. 121 and Table 8 (p. 122).

13. See 'The Cuban Economy in the Period 1959–63' in *UN Economic Survey of Latin America, 1963* (New York, 1965), pp. 259–89; Dudley Seers (ed.), *Cuba, the Economic and Social Revolution* (Chapel Hill, N.C. 1964), pp. 3–61; R. Blackburn in E. de Kadt (ed.), *Patterns of Foreign Influence in the Caribbean* (OUP/RIIA 1972), Chapter 7, 'Cuba and the Super-Powers'.

14. See UN *Yearbook of International Trade Statistics* 1960 (New York, 1962), p. 154.

15. Schreiber, p. 395.

16. Schreiber notes that "OAS sanctions were more a form of symbolic cooperation with the United States than an effective way of injuring Cuba . . . " Ibid., p. 389.

17. See A. R. M. Ritter, *The Economic Development of Revolutionary Cuba: Strategy and Performance* (1974), p. 96.

18. Ibid., p. 209.

19. See for instance Jorge I. Dominguez, *Cuba: Order and Revolution* (Harvard University Press, 1978).

20. Ritter claims that "for the latter years of the 1960s, the journalistic estimate of \$1 million aid per day (from the USSR) is probably an underestimate", op. cit., p. 210.

21. 'Viator', 'Cuba Revisited after Ten Years of Castro', *Foreign Affairs*, Vol. 48, 2, 1970, pp. 320–1.

22. Blackburn in de Kadt (ed.), p. 139.

23. See for instance, A. Uribe, *The Black Book of American Intervention in Chile* (Boston, 1974).

24. P. E. Sigmund, 'The "Invisible Blockade" and the Overthrow of Allende', *Foreign Affairs*, Vol. 52, 2, 1974, p. 326.

CHAPTER 4

1. Sir Anton Bertram, 'The Economic Weapon as a Form of Peaceful Pressure', 17 *Transactions of the Grotius Society*, (1932), 141. Bertram also summarized with prescience and accuracy the difficulties which would be encountered in any effort to apply economic sanctions to a 'delinquent' state.

2. Bertram, p. 169.

3. A. E. Hindmarsh, *Force in Peace* (1933), p. 160.

4. For an account of the Manchurian crisis see F. P. Walters, *A History of the League of Nations* (1960), 466ff.

5. See *ibid.*, 524ff; also W. R. Garner, *The Chaco Dispute* (1966).

6. For a brief list of works on the Italo-Ethiopian dispute see the Select Bibliography.

7. The vote for military measures was over 6.75 million. See Adelaide Livingstone's booklet *The Peace Ballot: the official history* (1935). See too Frank Hardie, *The Abyssinian Crisis* (1974), pp. 51–5.

8. For details of these sanctions see *Dispute Between Ethiopia and Italy*, Cmd. 5071 (London HMSO, 1936), pp. 43–50.

9. Hardie, p. 102.

10. See Walters, p. 670.

11. House of Lords *Debates*, Dec. 1935, Vol. 99, col. 352.

12. *The Report of the Committee of Experts for the Technical Examination of the Conditions Governing the Trade in and Transport of Petroleum and its Derivatives, By-Products and Residues* appears in *Dispute between Italy and Ethiopia*, Cmd. 5094 (London HMSO, 1936).

13. See Walters, p. 683; A. J. Toynbee, *Survey of International Affairs*, 1935, ii (1936), 463ff; Hardie, pp. 223–4, Lord Avon's comments are in *The Eden Memoirs, Facing the Dictators* (1962), pp. 384–5.

14. *The Economist*, 12 Oct. 1935, p. 694. For a contemporary account of the economic aspects of the sanctions experiment see H. V. Hodson's contribution to Toynbee's *Survey of International Affairs*, 1935, ii, 414ff.

15. See *The Economist*, 6 June 1936, p. 542.

16. Hodson, cited in n.14, p. 435.

17. M. J. Bonn commented: "The financial boycott did not imply much more than the moral sanctification of a prudent business-like attitude". 'How Sanctions Failed', *Foreign Affairs*, Vol. 15, 2 (1937), p. 354.

18. See Hodson, p. 434; *The Economist*, 18 Apr. 1936, p. 123.

19. P. Schmidt, *Hitler's Interpreter*, ed. R. H. C. Steed (1951), p. 60.

20. Mackenzie King to the Canadian House of Commons, 18 June 1936. See W. A. Riddell (ed.), *Documents on Canadian Foreign Policy 1917–1939* (Toronto, 1962), p. 575.

21. Lord Templewood (Sir Samuel Hoare) referred to support for this policy in his memoirs *Nine Troubled Years* (1954), 158 ff. See also Harold Macmillan *Winds of Change* (1966), Chapters 13–15.

22. See Walters, pp. 771–3.

23. For a detailed account of the League reform movement see S. Engel, *League Reform: an Analysis of official Proposals and Discussions, 1936–1939* (1940).

CHAPTER 5

1. Security Council Resolution 82, 25 June 1950.

2. Security Council Resolution 83, 27 June 1950.

3. General Assembly Resolution 500(V), 18 May 1951.

4. Security Council Resolutions 180, 31 July 1963 and 218, 23 Nov. 1965.

5. Originally the question of treatment of Indians in South Africa was a separate item on UN agenda, but it was merged with the general question of apartheid after 1952.

6. Good accounts of South Africa's external relations with neighbouring states can be found in K. W. Grundy, *Confrontation and Accommodation in Southern Africa: the limits of independence* (1973), and R. W. Johnson, *How Long Will South Africa Survive?* (1977). See too J. Barber, *South Africa's Foreign Policy 1945–1970* (1973).

7. See R. E. Bissell, *Apartheid and International Organizations* (1977).

8. Security Council Resolution 134, 1 Apr. 1960.

9. General Assembly Resolution 1761 (XVII), 6 Nov. 1962. The Afro-Asians and the Soviet bloc voted in favour; Latin American and most Scandinavian countries abstained; the US, Britain and the 'old' Commonwealth and Japan voted against.

10. Security Council Resolution 181, 7 Aug. 1963.

11. Security Council Resolution 182, 4 Dec. 1963.

12. UN Document S/6210, 2 Mar. 1965, SCOR 20th year, Special Supplement No. 2.

13. General Assembly Resolution 2145(XXI), 21 Oct. 1966. For the Court's judgment, see ICJ, *Report of Judgments, Advisory Opinions and Orders 1966*, p. 6. For an analysis of the judgment which damaged the reputation of the Court, particularly in third world estimation, see B. Cheng, 'The 1966 South West Africa Judgment of the World Court', 20 *Current Legal Problems* 1967, pp. 181–212.

14. Security Council Resolutions 276, 30 Jan. 1970, and 284, 29 July 1970.

15. ICJ *Reports*, 1971. The Legal Consequences for States of the continued presence of South Africa in Namibia, notwithstanding Security Council Resolution 276 (1970).

16. This date was later postponed. See below.

17. Security Council Resolution 418, 4 Nov. 1977. In Resolution 282 of 23 July 1970, the Security Council sought to strengthen the arms embargo by calling on states to withhold spare parts for vehicles and military equipment used by South African forces.

18. Rosalyn Higgins wrote in 1967 that "what constitutes an Article 39 situation is what you intend to do about it" ('International Law, Rhodesia and the UN', *The World Today*, Vol. XXIII, 1967, p. 102) and this appears to be the correct view, given the unwillingness of UN members to use the phraseology of Article 39 if sanctions are not planned. But two American commentators have suggested that "the two issues are entirely separable" and that a determination that a threat to the peace exists in South Africa – which they consider should be made by the Security Council – would not require "coterminous economic or military sanctions". Clyde Ferguson and William R. Cotter, 'South Africa: what is to be done', *Foreign Affairs*, Vol. 56, 2 1978, p. 268.

19. See R. C. Good, *UDI: The International Politics of the Rhodesian Rebellion* (1973); C. Palley, *The Constitutional History and Law of Rhodesia 1888–1965* (1966).

20. Once Zambia became independent, Southern Rhodesia (except in UN and some British government documents) was known as Rhodesia. In 1979 the government of Bishop Muzorewa renamed the country Zimbabwe-Rhodesia. 'Rhodesia' is used for consistency throughout this book.

21. Rhodesia: *Documents Relating to Proposals for a Settlement, 1966*, Cmnd. 3171 (London, 1966), p. 3.

22. House of Common *Debates*, 1 Nov. 1965, Vol. 718, coll. 633f.

23. Commonwealth Prime Ministers' Meeting in Lagos 1966: *Final Communique*, Cmnd. 2890 (London, 1966), p. 5.
24. General Assembly Resolution 2022(XX), 5 Nov. 1965.
25. Security Council Resolution 217, 20 Nov. 1965.
26. Security Council Resolution 221, 9 Apr. 1966.
27. Security Council Resolution 253, 29 May 1968.
28. The work of this Committee which has issued annual reports beginning in 1968 is discussed further in the next chapter.
29. Security Council Resolution 277, 18 Mar. 1970. No major additions to sanctions were made after this; but Security Council Resolution 333, 22 May 1973, authorized the Sanctions Committee to receive information about sanctions-breaking from individuals and non-governmental organizations.
30. The ups and downs of Rhodesian-South African relations are well chronicled in H. R. Strack, *Sanctions: The Case of Rhodesia* (1978). A low point was reached after the failure of the Victoria Falls Conference between Zambia and Rhodesia in August 1975; Mr. Smith was forced to apologize for criticizing South Africa's 'detente' policy. (Op. cit. pp. 72–74.)
31. The Central Statistical Office, Salisbury, gave the 1965 population as 4.3 million Africans; 210,000 whites; 13,400 other; in 1977 the figures were 6.5 million, 263,000 and 33,000.
32. For a variety of reasons certain states continued to trade with Rhodesia: South Africa, Portgual and its African provinces (till 1975), Switzerland, Botswana, Malawi, Zaire, Zambia. W. Germany imported graphite; the US chrome; Australia exported wheat. These are the 'reporting countries' referred to by the UN Secretariat; beyond this little is known about the extent of Rhodesian trade and estimates have a low degree of reliability.
33. Cases under investigation by the Security Council Sanctions Committee suggest widespread evasion of the embargoes; Strack suggests that in 1972 Rhodesia still accounted for 10 per cent of world trade in flue-cured tobacco. A suggestion by Britain that Bulgaria and the USSR were buying Rhodesian tobacco through an agent in Liechtenstein was indignantly denied by both governments. S/12529, Rev. I, Vol. I, *Tenth Report* of the UN Sanctions Committee, pp. 154, 161.
34. S/12529, Rev. I, Vol. II, p. 5.
35. For details of NCI (no currency involved) deals, see Strack, pp. 106–7.
36. See S/12579, Rev. I, Vol. I, p. 41. In 1965 visitors from abroad totalled 343,378; in 1975, 284,697; in 1976, 169,854.
37. S/12579, Rev. I, Vol. II, p. 14.
38. Martin Bailey and Bernard Rivers, *Oil Sanctions against Rhodesia*: a paper prepared for the Commonwealth Committee on Southern Africa (Commonwealth Secretariat, 1977). The authors acknowledge their principal information sources as (a) *'The Oil Conspiracy'* (N.Y. United Church of Christ, June 1976); (b) 'Submission to the British Government Inquiry on Allegations of Sanctions-Busting by Shell and British Petroleum' by the London-based Haslemere Group and Anti-Apartheid Movement (1977); (c) other letters and papers. Items (a) and (b) are printed in the Bailey-Rivers report as Attachments.

39. T. Bingham and S. M. Gray, *Report on the Supply of Petroleum and Petroleum Products to Rhodesia*, 1978 (Foreign and Commonwealth Office; HMSO).
40. See the *Bingham Report*, pp. 215–16.
41. Ibid., p. 217.
42. Ibid., p. 214.
43. See its *Sixth Report*, SCOR 29th year, Special Supplement, No. 2, S/11178, Rev. I, Case No. 144.
44. The 'Tango Romeo' case No. 154. The existence of this regular air freight service from Rhodesia first came to the Sanctions Committee's attention in 1972 and its ramifications are explored in all reports from the Sixth to the most recent (Tenth). In 1976 the government of Gabon reported that Affretair, the airline registered in Gabon which had been owned by Rhodesian interests had been dissolved and incorporated in Gabon's national airline. See 9th Report, SCOR 32nd year, Special Supplement No. 2, S/12265, Vol. I, p. 21. The whole story reads like a novel.
45. To quote one of many instances, the Greek government took two years to reply to the allegations that Greek ships were being used to transport sugar, suspected of being Rhodesian, from Mozambique to Kuwait.
46. *Sanctions: the Case of Rhodesia*, p. 96 (emphasis in original). Strack compares the Rhodesian economy to an automobile "stuck in low gear, slowly moving forward at full engine acceleration".

CHAPTER 6

1. J. Barber, 'Economic Sanctions as a Policy Instrument', *International Affairs*, Vol. 55, 3, 1979, pp. 367–384. Barber differentiates between three categories of objectives: 'primary' – concerned with the target state; 'secondary' – which relate to the "status, behaviour and expectations of the governments imposing the sanctions; 'tertiary' – "concerned with broader international considerations". (p. 370.)
2. The USSR rejected a trade agreement with the US and m.f.n. status because of the 'freedom of emigration' clause in the US Trade Act.
3. T. Bingham and S. M. Gray, *Report on the Supply of Petroleum . . . to Rhodesia* (*Bingham Report*), Foreign and Commonwealth Office, 1978, summary of evidence, p. 105.
4. A. E. Highley, *The First Sanctions Experiment: a study of League Procedures* (1938), p. 125.
5. M. Augustin Hamon's phrase is quoted by D. Mitrany, *The Problem of International Sanctions* (1925), p. 39.
6. Neutrality legislation passed in September 1935 obliged the United States government to assume a strictly impartial posture during the Italo-Ethiopian crisis. Arms were embargoed to both belligerents, and United States citizens were warned not to travel in ships owned by belligerents. The administration indicated a willingness to show a cooperative attitude towards the League by stating that its policy was to restrict trade to normal levels, and by advocating 'moral embargoes', but trade between the United States and Italy increased during the period of sanctions.

7. See SCOR 22nd year Supplement S/7781, pp. 117–18, for an official statement of the Swiss position.
8. *Bingham Report*, pp. 48–9.
9. See *International Sanctions: a Report by a Group of Members of the Royal Institute of International Affairs* (1938), where on p. 206 it is suggested that such assistance might have had a considerable effect.
10. See *The Front Line States: the Burden of the Liberation Struggle*, Commonwealth Secretariat, 1978, p. 1. An Appendix lists the reports of sundry UN review missions to Botswana and Mozambique.
11. Rhodesia closed the border on 9 January 1973 but not to copper. Zambia then stopped copper shipments over the border. Rhodesia reopened the border on 4 February, but Zambia decided to keep it closed.
12. Tanzania meets costs of maintenance of the Tazara line.
13. *The Front Line States*, p. 5.
14. Ibid., p. 34.
15. Ibid., p. 60.
16. Ibid., pp. 60–61.
17. League procedures in this crisis have been fully described. See particularly the work of A. E. Highley and E. Atwater in Section 3 of the Select Bibliography.
18. L. B. Pearson, 'Forty Years On: Reflections on our Foreign Policy', *International Journal*, Vol. 22, 3 (1967), p. 359.
19. See GAOR (VI) Supplement No. 13, UN Document A/1891; ibid (VII), Supplement No. 17, UN Document A/2215; ibid (IX), Annexes, Agenda item 19, UN Document A/2713–S/3283, pp. 1–4.
20. See L. Kapungu, *The United Nations and Economic Sanctions Against Rhodesia* (1973), pp. 48–51.
21. The Committee's work is recorded in a series of bulky reports; the first submitted in December 1968 (SCOR, 23rd year, Special Supplement S/8954), the most recent submitted in January 1979 (SCOR, 34th year, Special Supplement No. 2, Vol. I, S/13000).
22. In its 1977 Report the Committee recorded 21 cases opened on the basis of information from individuals and non-governmental organizations.
23. In 1977 the following were so listed: Belgium, Brazil, Gabon, the Ivory Coast, Liberia, Liechtenstein, Panama, Portugal, South Africa, Spain, Switzerland, Zaire. *Tenth Report*, SCOR, 33rd year Special Supplement No. 2, Vol. I S/12529 Rev. I, para. 14.
24. Ibid., para. 17.
25. Ibid., para. 22. See also *Fourth Report*, SCOR, 26th year, Special Supplement No. 2, S/10229. *Eighth Report*, SCOR, 31st year, Special Supplement No. 2, Vol. I, S/11927, Rev. I.
26. *Ninth Report*, SCOR, 32nd year, Special Supplement No. 2, Vol. I S/12265, para. 53.
27. Cf. the Gleneagles agreement concluded at the Commonwealth Heads of Government meeting in July 1977. Strack notes the double standard applies to Rhodesian sports teams, particularly their last minute exclusion from the 1972 Olympic Games which had a hardening effect on white opinion in Rhodesia and evoked some sympathy outside the country. *Sanctions: the case of Rhodesia*, Chapter 5, especially pp. 224–31.

28. See SCOR, 33rd year, *Tenth Report* of the Sanctions Committee, pp. 225–6, for ʼa report of this meeting.
29. Ibid.
30. See the next chapter for details of the oil supply arrangements. See also *Report of the Comptroller-General of the United States: Implementation of Economic Sanctions against Rhodesia* (Washington, D. C., 20 Apr. 1977) where the comment is made that a lack of emphasis in enforcing sanctions was attributable to the low priority assigned to it and a lack of sufficient personnel. (p. iii).
31. P. J. Kuyper, *The Implementation of International Sanctions: the Netherlands and Rhodesia* (Sijthoff, 1978).

CHAPTER 7

1. Cf. K. Waltz, *Theory of International Politics* (1979), p. 159. " . . . sustained economic sanctions against [the US] would amount to little more than self-mutilation for those imposing them".
2. F. P. Walters, *History of the League of Nations*, pp. 650–1.
3. See Wu Yuan-Li, *Economic Warfare* (1952), pp. 301–2.
4. *Peace and War* (1966), p. 406.
5. *Bingham Report* (1978), pp. 33–4.
6. M. Bailey and B. Rivers, *Oil Sanctions against South Africa* (UN, Centre against Apartheid: *Notes and Documents* 12/78, 1978), p. 7.
7. Ibid., pp. 46–9.
8. *Bigham Report*, pp. 38–40. See also *Oil Sanctions against Rhodesia*, pp. 10–11.
9. Bailey and Rivers, p. 52.
10. *South African Digest*, week ended 2 Mar. 1979.
11. S. Strange, 'The Strategic Trade Embargoes: Sense or Nonsense?', *Year Book of World Affairs*, Vol. 12 (1958), p. 66.
12. 'How Sanctions Failed', *Foreign Affairs*, Vol. 15, 2 (1937), p. 360.
13. UN Sanctions Committee *Tenth Report*, S/12529, Rev. 1, Vol. 1, p. 243.
14. See ibid., pp. 115–18.
15. *Oil Sanctions against Rhodesia* (Commonwealth Secretariat, 1978), p. 20.
16. '*The Oil Conspiracy*', published by the Center for Social Action of the United Church of Christ, 1976, reproduced as Attachment I in *Oil Sanctions against Rhodesia*.
17. *Oil Sanctions against Rhodesia*, p. 12.
18. Ibid., Attachment I, pp. 35–6, 39.
19. Ibid., pp. 36–8. It should be noted that in August 1977 President Kaunda brought suit against the oil companies for £4 billion damage, alleging they had starved Zambia of oil while supplying Rhodesia.
20. *Bingham Report*, p. iii.
21. Prepared by Messrs. Bailey and Rivers as previously cited.
22. *Bingham Report*, pp. iv–v.
23. See ibid., pp. 105–7, for an account of an interview on 21 February, 1968, between representatives of the Consolidated Group with George Thomson, Secretary of State for Commonwealth Relations.
24. Ibid., Chapters VIII and XIII.

25. H. Strack, *Sanctions: the case of Rhodesia*, p. 98.

26. *Data and analysis concerning the possibility of a US Food Embargo as a response to the present Arab oil boycott.* US 93rd Congress Committee Print, Congressional Research Service, 21 Nov. 1973 (Washington, D. C.) p. 1.

27. J. Galtung writes of the "naive theory" of the effects of economic warfare, which correlates value deprivation and political disintegration and "disregards the simple principle of adaptation . . .". 'On the Effects of International Economic Sanctions with Examples from the case of Rhodesia', *World Politics*, Vol. 19, Apr. 1967, p. 388.

28. G. W. Baer, 'Sanctions and Security. The League of Nations and the Italian-Ethiopian War 1935–1936'. *International Organization*, Vol. 27, 1973, p. 179.

29. Revelations in 1978 about the extent of the activities of the South African Department of Information brought the fall of a Minister (Mr. Mulder), the demise of the department and, in June 1979, the resignation of the State President, Mr. Vorster. It appears that public funds were used illegally in sundry transactions including an abortive attempt to buy leading newspapers inside and outside the Republic. At the time of writing, the full story is still unknown.

CHAPTER 8

1. H. C. Kelman has noted that sanctions play different roles in legitimized and non-legitimized contexts. See 'Patterns of Personal Involvement in the National System: a social-psychological analysis of political legitimacy' in J. N. Rosenau (ed.), *International Politics and Foreign Policy* (New York, 1969), p. 287n.

2. It is too soon to gauge the extent to which direct elections to the European Parliament will enhance the status of the European Community in the eyes of citizens of its member countries.

Select Bibliography

General Works

Books

Brownlie, Ian., *International law and the use of force by states* (London, OUP, 1963).

Clark, Evans, ed., *Boycotts and peace: a report by the Committee on Economic Sanctions* (New York, Harper for 20th Century Fund, 1932).

Hindmarsh, A. E., *Force in peace: force short of war in international relations* (Cambridge, Mass., Harvard UP, 1933).

Holland, Thomas H., *The mineral sanction as an aid to international security* (Edinburgh, Oliver and Boyd, 1935).

International sanctions: a report by a group of members of the Royal Institute of International Affairs (London, OUP for RIIA, 1938).

McDougal, Myres S. and F. P. Feliciano., *Law and minimum world public order: the legal regulation of international coercion* (New Haven, Conn., Yale UP, 1961).

Mitrany, David, *The problem of international sanctions* (London, OUP, 1925).

Ruzie, David, *Organisations internationales et sanctions internationales* (Paris, A. Colin, 1971).

Sanctions: the character of international sanctions and their application, 2nd rev. and enlarged ed. (London, Royal Institute of International Affairs, 1935). (Information Department Papers, no. 17.)

Webster, Charles, *Sanctions: the use of force in an international organisation* (London, David Davies Memorial Institute of International Studies, 1956). (Annual memorial lecture, 1956, DDMIIS.)

Wild, Payson S., *Sanctions and treaty enforcement* (Cambridge, Mass., Harvard UP, 1934).

Articles

Arens, Richard and Harold D. Lasswell, Towards a general theory of sanctions. 49 *Iowa Law Review* (1963–4), 233–276.

Arnold-Forster, W., Sanctions. *Journal of the Royal Institute of International Affairs*, vol. 5 (1926), 1–15.

Baldwin, David A., The power of positive sanctions. *World Politics*, vol. 24, 1 (1971), 19–38.

Barber, James, Economic sanctions as a policy instrument. *International Affairs*, vol. 55, 3 (July, 1979), 367–84.

Bertram, Anton, The economic weapon as a form of peaceful pressure. 17 *Transactions of the Grotius Society* (1931), 139–74.

Bowett, D., Economic Coercion and reprisals by states. *Virginia Journal of International Law*, vol. 13:1, (1972), 1–12.

Doxey, Margaret P., International sanctions: a framework for analysis with special reference to the UN and Southern Africa. *International Organization*, vol. 26:3 (1972), 527–550.

Doxey, Margaret P., Sanctions revisited. *International Journal*, vol. 31:1, (Winter 1975–76), 53–78.

Galtung, Johan, On the effects of international economic sanctions with examples from the case of Rhodesia. *World Politics*, vol. 19, 3 (April, 1967) 378–416.

Hoffmann, F., The function of economic sanctions: a comparative analysis. *Journal of Peace Research*, vol. 2 (1967), 140–159.

Holland, Thomas H., The mineral sanction as a contribution to international security. *International Affairs*, vol. 15 (Sept.-Oct. 1936), 735–52.

Lauterpacht, Hersch, Boycott in international relations. 14 *British Year Book of International Law* (1933), 125–40.

Lillich, Richard B., Economic coercion and the international legal order. *International Affairs*, vol. 51:3 (July 1975), 358–71.

Macdonald, R. St. J., The resort to economic coercion by international political organizations. 17 *University of Toronto Law Journal* (1967), 86–169.

Macdonald, R. St. J., Economic sanctions in the international system. 7 *Canadian Yearbook of International Law* (1969), 61–91.

Reisman, W. M., The enforcement of international judgments. 63 *American Journal of International Law* (1969), 1–27.

Sohn, L. B., Expulsion or forced withdrawal from an international organization. 77 *Harvard Law Review* (1964), 1381–1425.

Taubenfeld, Rita F., and Howard J. The 'economic weapon': the League and the United Nations. 58 *Proceedings of the American Society of International Law* (1964), 183–205. Also reprinted as a booklet.

Wallensteen, Peter, Characteristics of economic sanctions. *Journal of Peace Research*, 2 (1968), 248–67.

Williams, Benjamin H., The coming of economic sanctions into American practice. 37 *American Journal of International Law* (1943), 386–96.

Economic Warfare

Books

Adler-Karlsson, Gunnar, *Western economic warfare 1947–1967: a case study in foreign economic policy* (Stockholm, Almqvist & Wiksell, 1968).

Allen, Robert L., *Soviet economic warfare* (Washington, DC, Public Affairs Press, 1960).

Cohen, Jerome B., *Japan's economy in war and reconstruction* (Minneapolis, Univ of Minnesota Press, 1949).

Eckstein, Alexander, *Communist China's economic growth and foreign trade* (New York, McGraw Hill, 1966).

Gordon, D. L. and Royden Dangerfield, *The hidden weapon: the story of economic warfare* (New York, Harper, 1947).

Grebler, L. and W. Winkler, *The cost of the World War to Germany and to Austria-Hungary* (New Haven, Conn., Yale UP for Carnegie Endowment, 1940). (Economic and Social History of the World War, supplementary vols.)

Jack, D. T., *Studies in economic warfare* (London, King, 1940).

Medlicott, W. N., *The economic blockade* (London, HMSO and Longmans Green, i:1952; ii:1959. 2 vols). (History of the Second World War, UK Civil series.)

Medlicott, W. N., 'Economic warfare', in Arnold and Veronica M. Toynbee, eds, *Survey of International Affairs 1939–1946*, vii: *The war and the neutrals* (London, OUP for RIIA, 1956).

Ritchie, H., *The 'Navicert' system during the World War* (Washington, DC, Carnegie Endowment, 1938). (Monograph series, Division of International Law, no. 2.)

Salter, Arthur, *Allied shipping control: an experiment in international administration* (Oxford, Clarendon Press for Carnegie Endowment, 1921). (Economic and Social History of the World War, British series.)

Siney, Marion C., *The allied blockade of Germany, 1914–1916* (Ann Arbor, Univ. of Michigan Press, 1957).

Wolf, Thomas A., *US east-west trade policy* (Lexington, Mass., D.C. Heath, Lexington Books, 1973).

Wu, Yuan-li, *Economic warfare* (Englewood Cliffs, New Jersey, Prentice-Hall, 1952).

Articles

Allen, Robert L., State trading and economic warfare. 24 *Law and Contemporary Problems* (1959), 256–76.

Lee, Luke T. and John B. McCobb, "United States trade embargo on China, 1949–70: legal status and future prospects". *New York, University Journal of International Law and Politics*, vol. 4, 1 (Spring 1971), 1–28.

Polk, Judd, Freezing dollars against the Axis. *Foreign Affairs*, vol. 20, 1 (1941), 113–30.

Strange, Susan, The strategic trade embargoes: sense or nonsense? *Year Book of World Affairs*, vol. 12 (1958), 55–73.

Wilczynski, J., Strategic embargo in perspective. *Soviet Studies*, vol. 19:1 (1967), 74–86.

League of Nations Sanctions

Books

Atwater, Elton, *Administration of export and import embargoes by member states of the League of Nations, 1935–1936, with special reference to Great Britain, France, Belgium, the Netherlands, Denmark, Norway and Sweden* (Geneva, Geneva Research Centre, 1938). (Geneva Studies, 9/6.)

Baer, G. W., *The coming of the Italo-Ethiopian war* (Cambridge, Mass., Harvard UP, 1967).

Barker, A. J., *The civilizing mission: the Italo-Ethiopian war 1935–1936* (London, Cassell, 1968).

Barros, James, *The League of Nations and the great powers: the Greek-Bulgarian incident, 1925* (Oxford, Clarendon Press, 1970).

Buell, R. L., *The Suez canal and League sanctions* (Geneva, Geneva Research Centre, 1935). (Geneva Special Studies, 6/3.)

Engel, S., *League reform: an analysis of official proposals and discussions, 1936–1939* (Geneva, Geneva Research Centre, 1940). (Geneva Studies, 11/3–4.)

Feis, H., *Seen from E.A. [Economic Affairs]: three international episodes* (New York, Knopf, 1947).

Hardie, Frank, *The Abyssinian crisis* (London, Batsford, 1974).

Highley, Albert E., *The first sanctions experiment: a study of League procedures* (Geneva, Geneva Research Centre, 1938). (Geneva Studies, 9/4.)

Miller, D. H., *The drafting of the Covenant* (New York, Putnam, 1928). 2 vols.

Toynbee, Arnold J., *Survey of international affairs 1935, ii: Abyssinia and Italy* (London, OUP for RIIA, 1936).

Walters, F. P., *A history of the League of Nations* (London, OUP, 1952, 2 vols; 1960, reprinted in 1 vol.).

Articles

Bonn, M. J., How sanctions failed. *Foreign Affairs*, vol. 15, 2 (1937), 350–61.

Baer, George W., "Sanctions and security: the League of Nations and the Italian-Ethiopian War, 1935–1936". *International Organization*, vol. 27, 2 (1973), 165–80.

Bradley, Phillips, Some legislative and administrative aspects of the application of Article XVI of the Covenant. 22 *Transactions of the Grotius Society* (1936), 13–29.

Hubbard, Ursula P., The cooperation of the United States with the League of Nations, 1931–1936. *International Conciliation*, no. 329 (Apr. 1937), 293–468.

Sanctions in the Italo-Ethiopian conflict. *International Conciliation*, no. 315 (Dec. 1935), 539–44.

Williams, John Fischer, Sanctions under the Covenant. 17 *British Year Book of International Law* (1936), 130–49.

Wright, Quincy, The test of aggression in the Italo-Ethiopian war. 30 *American Journal of International Law* (1936), 45–57.

Zimmern, Alfred, The League's handling of the Italo-Abyssinian dispute. *International Affairs*, vol. 14 (Nov.-Dec. 1935), 751–68.

United Nations Sanctions

Books

Arnold, Guy et al., *Sanctions against Rhodesia 1965 to 1972* (London, Africa Bureau, May 1972, mimeographed).

Bailey, Martin and Bernard Rivers, *Oil sanctions against Rhodesia.* A paper prepared for the Commonwealth Committee on Southern Africa (London, Commonwealth Secretariat, 1977).

Barber, James, *South Africa's foreign policy: 1945–1970* (London, OUP, 1973).

Bingham, T. H. and S. M. Gray, *Report on supply of petroleum and petroleum products to Rhodesia* (London, HMSO, Sept. 1978), (Foreign and Commonwealth Office).

Bissell, Richard E., *Apartheid and international organizations* (Boulder, Co., Westview Press, 1977).

Curtin, Timothy and David Murray, *Economic sanctions and Rhodesia: an examination of the probable effect of sanctions on national and personal incomes in Rhodesia and of the effectiveness of sanctions on Rhodesian policy* (London, Institute of Economic Affairs, 1967). (Research Monographs, no. 12.)

Doxey, Margaret P., *Economic sanctions: past lessons and the case of Rhodesia* (Canadian Institute of International Affairs, Toronto, 1968). (Behind the Headlines series, 29/2.)

Dugard, John, *The South West Africa/Namibia dispute: documents and scholarly writings on the controversy between South Africa and the United Nations* (Berkeley, Univ. of California Press, 1973).

Good, Robert C., *U.D.I.: The international politics of the Rhodesian rebellion* (London, Faber, 1973).

Grundy, K. W., *Confrontation and accommodation in Southern Africa: the limits of independence* (Berkeley, Univ. of California Press, 1973).

Gyeke-Dako, K., *Economic sanctions under the United Nations* (Tema, Ghana, Ghana Publishing Corp., 1973).

Kapungu, Leonard, *The United Nations and economic sanctions against Rhodesia* (Lexington, Mass., D.C. Heath, 1973).

Kuyper, Pieter J., *The implementation of international sanctions: the Netherlands and Rhodesia* (Alphen aan der Rijn, Sijthoff and Noordhoff, 1978).

Lake, Anthony, *The 'Tar Baby' option: American policy towards Southern Rhodesia* (New York, Columbia UP, 1976).

Leiss, Amelia, ed., *Apartheid and United Nations collective measures: an analysis* (New York, Carnegie Endowment, 1965).

Segal, Ronald, ed., *Sanctions against South Africa* (International Conference on Economic Sanctions against South Africa), (Harmondsworth, Penguin Books, 1964).

Spence, J. E., *Republic under pressure: a study of South African foreign policy* (London, OUP for RIIA, 1965). (Chatham House Essays, no. 9.)

Strack, Harry R., *Sanctions: the case of Rhodesia* (Syracuse New York, Syracuse UP, 1978).

Sutcliffe, R. B., *Sanctions against Rhodesia: the economic background* (London, Africa Bureau, 1966).

United States House Committee on Foreign Affairs, Subcommittee on International organizations and movements. *Sanctions as an instrumentality of the United Nations: Rhodesia as a case study* (Washington, DC, G.P.O., 1972).

Zacklin, Ralph, *The United Nations in Rhodesia: a study in international law* (New York, Praeger, 1974).

Articles

Barber, James and Michael Spicer, Sanctions against South Africa – options for the west. *International Affairs*, vol. 55, 3 (1979), 385–401.

Dale, Richard, South Africa and the international community. *World Politics*, 18/2 (1966), 297–313.

Doxey, Margaret P., The Rhodesian sanctions experiment. *Year Book of World Affairs*, vol. 25 (1971), 142–62.

Ferguson, Clyde and William R. Cotter, "South Africa: what is to be done"? *Foreign Affairs*, vol. 52, 2 (1978), 253–74.

Goodrich, L. M., Korea: collective measures against aggression. *International Conciliation*, no. 494 (Oct. 1953), 129–92.

Haldermann, J. W., Some legal aspects of sanctions in the Rhodesian case. *International and Comparative Law Quarterly*, 17, part 3 (July 1968), 672–705.

Higgins, Rosalyn, International law, Rhodesia, and the UN. *World Today*, 23/3 (1967), 94–106.

Kelsen, Hans, Sanctions under the charter of the United Nations. *Canadian Journal of Economics and Political Science*, 12/4 (Nov. 1946), 429–38.

McDougal, Myres S. and Michael Reisman, Rhodesia and the United Nations: the lawfulness of international concern. 62 *American Journal of International Law*, (1968), 1–19.

McKinnell, R. T., Sanctions and the Rhodesian economy. *Journal of Modern African Studies*, 7/4 (1969), 559–81.

Mudge, G. A., Domestic policies and UN activities: the cases of Rhodesia and the Republic of South Africa. *International Organizations*, vol. 21 (Winter 1967), 55–78.

Sutcliffe, R. B., The political economy of Rhodesian sanctions. *Journal of Commonwealth Political Studies*, 7/2 (July 1969), 113–25.

Williams, Michael and Michael Parsonage. Britain and Rhodesia: the economic background to sanctions. *The World Today*, vol. 29:9 (Sept. 1973), 379–388.

Zacklin, R., Challenge of Rhodesia. *International Conciliation*, no. 575 (Nov. 1969), 5–72.

OAS Sanctions

Books

Chayes, Abram, *The Cuban missile crisis: International crisis and the role of law* (London, OUP, 1974).

Connell-Smith, G., *The inter-American system* (London, OUP, 1966).

Lieuwen, Edwin, *United States policy in Latin America* (New York, Praeger, 1965).

Logan, R. W., *Haiti and the Dominican Republic* (OUP for RIIA, 1968).

Ritter, Archibald R. M., *The economic development of revolutionary Cuba: strategy and performance* (New York, Praeger, 1974).

Seers, Dudley, ed., *Cuba: the economic and social revolution* (Chapel Hill, Univ. of North Caroline Press, 1964).

Slater, Jerome R., *Intervention and negotiation: the United States and the Dominican revolution* (London, Harper, 1970).

Slater, J., *The OAS and United States foreign policy* (Columbus, Ohio State UP, 1967).

Suárez, Andrés, *Cuba: Castroism and communism, 1959–1966*, tr. J. Carmichael and E. Halperin (Cambridge, Mass., MIT Press, 1967).

Articles

Akehurst, Michael, Enforcement action by regional agencies with special reference to the Organization of American States. *British Yearbook of International Law*, (1967), 173–227.

Berner, W. W., Soviet strategy towards Cuba, Latin America and the Third World. *Bulletin* (Munich, Institute for the Study of the USSR), 15/7 (July 1968), 3–12.

Claude, Inis L., Jr., The OAS, the UN, and the United States. *International Conciliation*, no. 547 (Mar. 1964), 3–67.

Macdonald, R. St. J., The Organization of American States in action. 15 *University of Toronto Law Journal* (1964), 325–429.

Miller, Linda, Regional organization and the regulation of internal conflict. *World Politics* 19/4 (1967), 582–600.

Schreiber, Anna P., Economic coercion as an instrument of foreign policy: US economic measures against Cuba and the Dominican Republic. *World Politics* 25/3 (1973), 387–412.

Slater, J., The limits of legitimization in international organization: the Organization of American States and the Dominican crisis. *International Organization*, 23/1 (1969), 48–72.

Tretiak, Daniel, Cuba and the Soviet Union: the growing accommodation, 1964–1965. *Orbis*, 11/2 (1967), 439–58.

Walters, R. S., Soviet economic aid to Cuba 1959–1964. *International Affairs*, 42/1 (Jan. 1966), 74–86.

Wiesel, I., The Cuban economy after the Revolution. *Acta Oeconomica* (Budapest), 3/2 (1968), 203–220.

Viator, Cuba revisited after ten years of Castro. *Foreign Affairs*, 48/2 (1970), 312–321.

Arab League Boycotts

Books

Casadio, Gien Paolo, *The economic challenge of the Arabs* (London, Saxon House: D.C. Heath, 1976).

Chill, D. S., *The Arab boycott of Israel: economic aggression and world reaction* (New York, Praeger, 1976).

Iskander, Marwan, *The Arab oil question* (Beirut, M. E. Economic Consultants, 1974).

Iskander, Marwan, *The Arab boycott of Israel* (Beirut, Research Center, Palestine Liberation Organization, 1966). (Palestine Monographs, no. 6.)

Khalil, Muhammad, *The Arab states and the Arab League: a documentary record* (London, Constable, 2 vols., 1962).

Macdonald, Robert, *The League of Arab States: a study in dynamics of regional organization* (Princeton, NJ, Princeton Univ. Press, 1965).

Maull, Harris, *Oil and influence: the oil weapon examined* (London, International Institute for Strategic Studies, Adelphi Papers, no. 117, 1975).

Moore, John Norton, *United States policy and the Arab boycott* (American Society of International Law, proceedings, 1977, 174–182).

Paust, Jordan J. and Albert P. Blaustein, *The Arab oil weapon* (New York, Dobbs Ferry, Oceana, 1977).

Shamsedin, Ezzedin M., *Arab oil and the United States: an admixture of politics and economics* (Columbia, S.C., Univ. of South Carolina, 1974). (Bureau of Business and Economic Research, Essays in Economics, no. 29.)

United States House Committee on Foreign Affairs: *Data and analysis concerning the possibility of a US food embargo as a response to the present Arab oil boycott.* 93rd congress, 1st session, Washington, DC, (Nov. 21, 1973).

United States Library of Congress: Congressional Research Service: *Oil fields as military objectives: a feasibility study.* House Committee on Inter-Relations: Special Subcommittee on Investigations, Committee Print, Washington, DC, G.P.O., 1975.

Articles

Paust, Jordan J. and Albert P. Blaustein, The Arab oil weapon – a threat to international peace. 68 *American Journal of International Law* (1974), 410–39.

Rostow, Eugene V., The illegality of the Arab attack on Israel of October 6, 1973. 69 *American Journal of International Law* (1975), 272–89.

Shihata, Ibrahim, Destination embargo of Arab oil: its legality under international law. 68 *American Journal of International Law* (1974), 591–627.

Singer, S. Fred, Limits to Arab oil power. *Foreign Policy*, no. 30 (Spring 1978), 53–67.

Tucker, Robert W., Oil: the issue of American intervention. *Commentary* (Jan. 1975), 21–31.

COMECON Boycotts

Books

Clissold, Stephen, ed., *A short history of Jugoslavia to 1966* (London, CUP, 1966).
Farrell, R. B., *Jugoslavia and the Soviet Union 1948–1956* (Hamden, Conn., Shoestring Press, 1956).
Kaser, Michael, *COMECON: integration problems of the planned economies* (2nd ed. London, OUP for RIIA, 1967).

Articles

Rusinow, Dennison I., Yugoslav development between East and West. *Journal of International Affairs*, 19/2 (1965), 181–193.

Index